Perfect Exterior
STAINING

QUARRY

Perfect Exterior
STAINING

A Step-by-Step Guide to Selecting and Applying
Beautiful Wood Finishes • Tom Philbin

GLOUCESTER MASSACHUSETTS

QUARRY BOOKS

First published in the United States of America by
Quarry Books, an imprint of
Rockport Publishers, Inc.
33 Commercial Street
Gloucester, Massachusetts 01930-5089
Telephone: (978) 282-9590
Fax: (978) 283-2742
www.rockpub.com

Library of Congress Cataloging-in-Publication Data

Philbin, Tom, [date]
    Perfect exterior staining : a step-by-step guide to selecting and applying beautiful stain finishes / Tom Philbin.
        p.   cm.
    ISBN 1-59253-073-7 (pbk.)
    1. Wood finishing. 2. Stains and staining. I. Title.
    TT325.P47 2004
    684'.084—dc22   2004002787

ISBN 1-59253-073-7

10 9 8 7 6 5 4 3 2 1

Design: Leigh Mantoni Stewart
Cover Images: Front Cover: All photos by Brian Vanden Brink
Design credits: Jim Sterling, Architect, (top right);
    Horiuchi & Solien Landscape Architects, (second from top, right);
    Winton Scott, Architect, (middle left); Mark Hutker & Associates Architects,
    (bottom left); South Mountain Company Builders, (second from left, bottom);
    Centerbrook Architects, (second from right, bottom)
Back cover: All photos by Brian Vanden Brink
Design credits: Scott Simons, Architect, (top); Rob Whitten, Architect,
    (middle); Roc Caivano, Architect, (bottom)

Stain is a safe product if used properly and if the precautions and instructions provided by the manufacturer are followed. Make sure you protect yourself by reading and following instructions and precautions on all stain and equipment to be used. The author and publisher assume no responsibility, legal or otherwise, for accidents, material exposure, equipment failure, or less-than-expected aesthetic outcomes.

Printed in Singapore

> Contents

Introduction

This book is designed to show do-it-yourselfers why and how to stain and restain exterior wood. It is difficult to believe, but there are no other books exclusively devoted to this topic available. This book finally fills the need for this information.

In many areas of the country, exterior stain is not only more commonly used than exterior paint, it is the only practical way to protect and add beauty and years of life to certain types of exterior wood. Decks, for example, should be coated but paint is impractical—mainly because it peels. Many types of fence are better stained than painted, and the same is true of exterior furniture and wood sidings, such as cedar and redwood. It makes little sense to install beautiful cedar and redwood siding and then cover its beauty with paint.

This book is also needed because of the lack of good information available about exterior stains and staining. I saw undeniable evidence of this when I worked part-time in the paint department of a large home improvement center. I was peppered daily with questions on exterior stains and staining—regarding application, the benefits of stain versus paint, whether it's a value economically—and the queries came from do-it-yourselfers and professional painters alike. In addition, I heard myths, for example, that you shouldn't coat new wood quickly but rather let it "weather" so it accepts finishes better. (Wrong—as it weathers it deteriorates.) I hope to illustrate not only how to—but how not to—use exterior stains.

Good luck!

—Tom Philbin

CHAPTER 1

Stains and Staining

Fifteen or twenty years ago, if you wanted to protect the exterior wood surfaces of your home, you only had one choice: paint. But that has changed dramatically with the proliferation of exterior stains for wood. Aside from the aesthetic appeal of a natural-looking finish, in many cases, stains have decidedly practical advantages over paint.

Paints and stains do share common characteristics. They are both designed to protect wood against the ravages of weather, and both can be used on all kinds of wood structures—the house itself, furniture, fencing, sheds, gazebos, and more. Both products make wood last years longer.

Paint and stain differ in various ways as well. One factor is the look: Paint provides a dense, opaque, film-forming finish, a colored skin that totally obscures the color and grain of the wood. In general, stain penetrates the wood like sauce penetrates sponge cake, usually up (or literally speaking, down) to a depth of $\frac{1}{8}$ inch (0.3 cm), depending on the wood species and condition. Paint bonds to wood as a film with little or no penetration.

In summary, paints and solid-color stains cover wood with a film and are therefore known as film-forming finishes. Stains penetrate the wood and are known as penetrating finishes.

OPPOSITE **If you stain the floor of a porch or other protected shelter you can expect longer life for the stain because it will not be subject to the direct onslaught of sun and rain.**

Varying Degrees of Transparency

Stain comes in varying degrees of transparency. Some allow color and grain to show through completely; others provides a semitransparent coating that allows only the grain to show through, and others cover in the same opaque way that paint covers, but because stain is much thinner than paint, surface texture shows through.

In terms of disadvantages, paint lasts longer than stain. According to studies done by the Forest Products Laboratory, a unit of the U.S. Department of Agriculture, paints last an average of seven years before recoating is required, whereas stains last anywhere from a year to five years, depending on the type of stain and its quality.

A big advantage that stain has over paint, however, is its ease of application. It's much lighter than paint (it has much more thinner, or solvent, in it), and you don't have to worry about smoothing it out like paint. However, in some cases you do have to be concerned with lap marks and over-application.

Perhaps the greatest advantage that stain has is in preparing the surface—or, more precisely, not having to prepare it. When the stain fades and it is time to apply a fresh coat, preparation time is virtually nonexistent. You just make sure the wood is clean and start applying the material.

Compare that to preparing paint for recoating. If the paint is peeling, the peeled areas must be scraped clean, sanded down, primed, and then painted. Hours, even days, are ordinarily involved.

In general, four kinds of exterior stain are available: clear, toner, semitransparent, and solid color. Let's take a closer look at each.

Clear Coatings

For people who want to retain the natural color, texture, and pattern of wood as much as possible, a penetrating clear coating is the way to go. When applied to the wood, it obscures color and grain about as much as pouring water on it would. I should clarify that I am referring to clear coatings that penetrate the wood, not polyurethanes or marine varnishes, which don't. For more on this topic, see the sidebar "A No-No: Using Clear Films Outdoors," on page 22. Clear, penetrating coatings don't crack. Instead, they penetrate into the wood fibers and coat them with chemicals that repel water.

The most important quality a coating has in making wood last is its ability to repel water. Nothing damages wood more quickly or more severely than water. If the water can get to unprotected fibers, it will cause them to swell like a sponge. Then, when the wood dries, it shrinks. When this process is repeated—gets wet and swells, dries and shrinks—over and over again, it creates a bellows effect, a drying and wetting cycle, and stresses the wood, which may warp or crack.

Liquid water, defined as that supplied by rain and snow, is the main cause of this type of damage. On decks, for example, deck boards are not normally coated on the underside. Water vapor (evaporation) does come up from the ground, but this isn't water about which you need to be concerned.

Some clear coatings protect against water only, and if that's all you want to do, fine. But be aware that mildew, a fungal growth, can gradually turn wood

BELOW **When water is being repelled from wood, it usually beads when it hits the surface, but some manufacturers say beading is not required to prove repellency.**

BELOW **If you like the natural look of wood, choose a clear stain. It allows the color and grain of the wood to show though. Here you see a deck partially coated with clear stain.**

gray and can create unsightly blotches. In addition, clear coatings last only a relatively short time, approximately a year. On the other hand, these products are usually affordable, costing under $10 a gallon.

Preservatives: Protecting against Fungus and Insects

In all but the most dire desert climates, you should choose a coating that contains a preservative—mildewcides and fungicides—to protect wood against the formation of mildew or other fungi. Fungi need water to grow.

Some confusion exists about preservatives. These chemicals do not make wood last longer; they just protect against fungi and insects. Also, note that not all clear sealers contain preservatives. (In the United States, using the word preservative on the label involves an expensive registration process with the Environmental Protection Agency.) Some companies may use claims such as "preserves wood" but also "resists mildew" or "mildew resistant" to try to get the message across without using the exact term. In some cases the expensive words "wood preservative" are used. Be sure to check with the manufacturer directly if you want or need more specific information.

Ultraviolet Rays

If you want to use a clear stain while also providing protection against the sun, it means protecting against ultraviolet (UV) rays. UV rays destroy the lignin, the "glue" that holds the wood fibers together, and if the wood is of poor quality, the sun can warp and crack it.

To protect against UV rays, buy a clear stain with UV blockers. Although these chemicals are transparent to the naked eye, they are opaque to UV rays.

Two kinds of UV blocker are available. One kind, a UV absorber, acts like an energy absorber. One expert compares them to a guitar string. When the UV ray hits the absorber, the absorber vibrates and dissipates the energy before it can do any harm to the wood structure. Unfortunately, these chemicals tend to break down rather quickly, and don't protect as well after that.

Much better are clear stains that contain what are known as trans oxide UV blockers. These blockers contain metals that have been ground to microscopic size. When the UV ray hits the metal, it is reflected. Trans oxide UV blockers are not cheap, but they do the job.

ABOVE **On this home, semi-transparent stain was applied to the cedar siding, and the trim was finished with green paint.**

You can tell if a clear coating contains UV blockers—though you won't be able to tell what kind—if you check the label. It should say that the product protects against "UV rays of the sun" or something similar. Call the manufacturer's toll free number to find out what kind of UV blockers they use.

Can You Walk on It?

If you intend to use the clear coating on a deck, make sure the label clearly states that it is formulated for that use. Coatings contain chemicals called resins, and some make the product suitable to be walked on and some do not.

Toners

Some clear coatings contain a slight amount of pigment and are known as toners. Like clear glass that contains a little green or brown colorant that renders it green or brown glass, both clear coatings and toners are still transparent.

Toners come in various hues. The most popular are the earth colors—browns, blacks, reds, blues, and greens—but lighter colors such as beige and white are also available. Toners allow the grain and the texture of the wood to show through while providing some color. The pigment also blocks UV rays. Some toners also contain mildewcides and fungicides; if they do, their label should say so.

These products are good to use if you want the wood to have just a hint of color, or if you want to make a less-expensive wood, such as pressure-treated pine, look like a more elegant wood, like cedar or redwood.

Semitransparent Stains

Semitransparent stains contain enough pigment to make them partially opaque and, therefore, more resistant to damage from the sun. Visually, they reveal less of the wood's grain and texture. Like

RIGHT **Close-up of semitransparent stain being applied to a deck. Note how the stain allows the grain of the wood to show through.**

ABOVE **From left to right: uncoated board, board coated with clear coating, then toner, semitransparent, semi-solid, and solid-color stains. Penetrating stains look different on different woods.**

> Why Finish Wood at All?

Some people wonder why wood should be finished at all. After all, some wooden structures have lasted hundreds of years. This is true, however not all wooden structures, left unfinished, will last hundreds of years. Some of them, depending on the weather and the wood itself, develop rot and deteriorate to the point of collapse.

Another consideration is appearance. If you want natural wood to retain its color, you're out of luck. Sunlight turns all woods yellowish or brownish, then gray. After the initial color change and graying, further changes develop slowly. Dark woods eventually become lighter and light woods darker. But damage—from sun and water, which gets into the wood and makes it alternately expand and contract as it goes through wetting and drying cycles—can lead to surface checks, which then develop into cracks. The grain raises and loosens, the boards cup and sometimes warp, and the wood becomes friable, with fragments separating from the surface.

Then there is mildew, which, as mentioned earlier, is a fungus that grows on wood, particularly in moist climates. Eventually, mildew will cover a surface, making it look gray or black. The problem is that on the way to a uniform gray or black color—if you like that—the wood takes on a blotchy look. In and of itself mildew is not dangerous, but it surely doesn't look good.

> You don't need a product with a preservative in it if your deck is made of CCA, or pressure-treated wood, which is wood injected with chromated copper arsenate. Many decks are made of it, and its replacement—not available at the time of writing—will contain a preservative other than arsenate. Note: This type of wood was recently banned in the United States (as of December 2003), and has already been banned in all fifteen European Union countries, because of the dangers associated with arsenic. For more on the issues surrounding pressure-treated woods, see page 110.

toners, semitransparent stains are available in earth tones as well as several other colors.

Penetrating stains (clear coatings, toners, and semitransparent stains) work because they soak into the wood. Therefore, they don't work well on composite materials such as hardboard, flakeboard, or oriented strand board. These materials are manufactured with glues, waxes, and additives that do not have the open structure of regular wood and, therefore, cannot be penetrated. The stain dries on the surface of the product as a film and eventually peels off.

VOCs

Penetrating stains rely on solvents to draw water repellents into the wood. Many experts favor traditional oil- and mineral-spirits–based sealers for their proven ability to penetrate wood. However, these formulations release VOCs, or volatile organic compounds, which deplete the ozone or increase smog.

Many regions have established legal limits on the amount of VOCs a product can release, commonly 250 grams per gallon. To comply with this regulation, many manufacturers strive to create formulations that do not rely heavily on high-VOC solvents. For oil-based formulations, manufacturers frequently decrease the solvent and increase the solid content of the stain. However, this practice can lead to the sealer not being able to penetrate the wood to the degree it should. It can also make the product harder to apply.

Another approach manufacturers have taken to comply with VOC laws is the use of modified oil emulsions, which break down oil into droplets small enough to suspend in water. This solution eliminates most of the harmful solvents and allows soap-and-water cleanup, but it also, some people say, reduces the stain's ability to penetrate the wood.

The newest product in the battle to reduce VOCs is the water-based acrylic coating. These clear coatings are easy to apply, and they can be cleaned up with soap and water. However, acrylics tend to form a film on the wood surface that is vulnerable to the destructive effects of sunlight and abrasive foot traffic. But manufacturers are continuing to develop other formulations, and some say that the products they're developing work fine.

Right now, it is impossible to give absolute, clear guidelines on how buyers can protect themselves and get the best possible products because some manufacturers, in their zeal to sell their product, say virtually anything about the product, as long as it's positive. For years, oil-based penetrating stains were considered to be superior to water-based ones. My personal feeling is that they still are. However, environmental concerns should be considered when making your choice.

> **Tip: Different Rates of Weathering**
No matter the finish applied to a house, different sides of the structure weather at different rates and may not have to be finished every time you apply a stain (or paint). Normally, the north side of a building weathers the slowest.

OPPOSITE **The trim color should work in harmony with siding color. Here, the reddish-orange color is markedly different but works because it's in the same warm-brown color family.**

ABOVE **Here, gray solid-color stain was used on the siding and paint was used on the trim. Solid-color stain is essentially flat paint.**

BELOW **Solid-color stain is also formulated for surfaces that are walked on. Make sure the package label specifies this characteristic before buying it for a deck.**

> Tip: Watch the Temperature

Don't apply a stain if the temperature is below what the manufacturer recommends. You can encounter problems if you ignore this advice.

Solid-Color Stain

Some people claim that solid-color stain is not a stain at all, that it's a thin paint, and a case can be made for that stance. Like paint, solid-color stains come in solid colors that obscure the wood and, like paint, can peel, though they are much more likely to simply wear off of the surface.

Solid-color stains are available in oil- and latex-acrylic–based formulations. Acrylics are better products than oil-based stains primarily because they are less likely to peel. In any film-building coating, the acrylic polymers used are more elastic and adhere to the surface better than oil-based polymers, which are more brittle and tend to crack.

For many years, manufacturers formulated solid-color stains for use only on vertical services such as siding and fencing, because they could not be made durable enough to stand up to foot traffic. Today, a number of manufacturers say that the acrylic resins used in the stain are strong enough to stand up to foot traffic and furniture and whatever else might be dragged across the deck.

Solid-color stains come in a rainbow of colors. In fact, color seems to be the prime consideration of buyers today. According to a study by one manufacturer, fifty-eight percent of all stain buyers buy solid-color satins.

You can get a longer life from a solid-stain application by using multiple coats. In fact, for woods such as cedar, cypress, and redwood, manufacturers recommend that you use a stain-blocking primer under the stain. The primer prevents tannins—blackish brown extractives that migrate to the wood surface—from discoloring the finish. However, clear coatings, toners, or semitransparent stains might be a better choice for beautiful woods such as redwood or cedar anyway. But solid-color stain is certainly an option.

BELOW **Here, a concrete house features muted colors, with steps and floors stained with a contrasting terra-cotta color.**

Semi-solid

Few companies make semi-solid stain. It contains more pigment than semitransparent stain but less than solid-color stain, and when applied, the wood grain is still visible. The benefit of a semi-solid stain is that additional pigment means more protection for the wood against the sun. Like semitransparent stains, semi-solid stains come in a wide variety of colors.

> Tip: Colors That Harmonize

When you select stains for use on and around the house, make sure they harmonize with one another. Manufacturers provide booklets with suggested color combinations that work well together. You can also refer to the palettes starting on page 26, which offer inspirational color combinations.

> Buying Tips

Sometimes you can achieve significant savings on exterior toners or semitransparent stains. The best time of year to buy them is usually mid autumn. Stain is composed of a pigment and a solvent. If the cans have been on shelves over the winter, the pigment settles to the bottom and can be difficult to mix in the spring. Dealers want to unload it, thus the fall sales.

Buy your product and then store it upside down, so the pigment on the bottom can redistribute itself throughout the can. You can also usually save by buying stain—assuming you can use it—in five-gallon containers rather than in gallons or quarts. Ideally, plan the job so you don't have to buy quarts, which are priced the highest.

Weathering Stain

Some companies also make what is known as weathering stain. It works by turning wood gray, as if it were aging and mildewed. Many people like this look but not the damage that goes along with it when it is happening naturally.

Bleaching Oil

This product can be applied on new wood like a whitewash. Whereas it does protect wood from water and UV rays, it contains chemicals that turn the wood fibers gray over six to twelve months. If you want, you can mix weathering stain and bleaching oil together—but you should check with the manufacturer to see if they're compatible.

Concrete Stain

Another type of stain that can have some great uses around the home is concrete stain. This acrylic product can be used to perk up exterior surfaces, such as driveways, steps, walkways, and even garage floors. Concrete stains come in a wide variety of colors, including custom-mixed, and are easy to apply with a short-napped roller. Chapter seven has more details.

> Tip: Using Paint on Trim

Many people prefer to have a gloss or semigloss look on trim, so they use paint because solid-color stain comes only in flat. It should be noted, however, that when it comes time to repaint, chances are that there will be more preparation involved in getting the surface ready for painting than for solid-color staining.

BELOW **Peeling varnish on exterior wood. Clear coatings such as varnish and polyurethane should not be used outdoors because they will usually peel.**

> A No-No: Using Clear Films Outdoors

Ever drive through a neighborhood and sees an entry door or wooden garage door with a bleached look? It's usually the result of someone having used a clear film, such as spar varnish, marine varnish, or polyurethane on the door.

Clear coatings such as spar urethane or marine varnish are film-forming finishes and are not generally recommended for use on exterior wood. The sun is the main problem. Ultraviolet rays penetrate the transparent film and degrade the wood underneath it. Regardless of the number of coats applied, the finish eventually becomes brittle and develops severe cracks and peels—often in less than two years. Photochemically degraded wood fibers peel from the wood along with the finish. If the finish does not require a long service life or is protected from direct sunlight by an overhang or porch, then the north side of a structure can be coated with exterior-grade varnish. In these areas, a minimum of three coats is recommended, and the wood should first be treated with a water-repellent preservative. The use of colored stains or sealers that are compatible with the varnish also makes it last longer. In marine exposures, six coats of varnish should be applied for better performance.

Two-part polyurethane, another clear coating, does not work well in exterior applications. These coatings are tougher and more resistant to ultraviolet rays than other film-forming transparent coatings, but they are expensive and difficult to use and usually have as short a life as conventional varnishes.

The other clear coatings, lacquer and shellac, are not suitable for outdoor use because they have little resistance to moisture, are brittle, and crack easily.

Applying Stain

Other chapters in the book detail how to apply stain, but in general (except for solid-color stain) a brush is the best applicator because it drives the products into the wood pores better than other applicators. But rollers, pads, garden sprayers, and power sprayers can also be used, depending on the product and the surface being coated. Again, follow the manufacturer's instructions.

BELOW **This color wheel shows the range of colors and degrees of transparency of current staining products.**

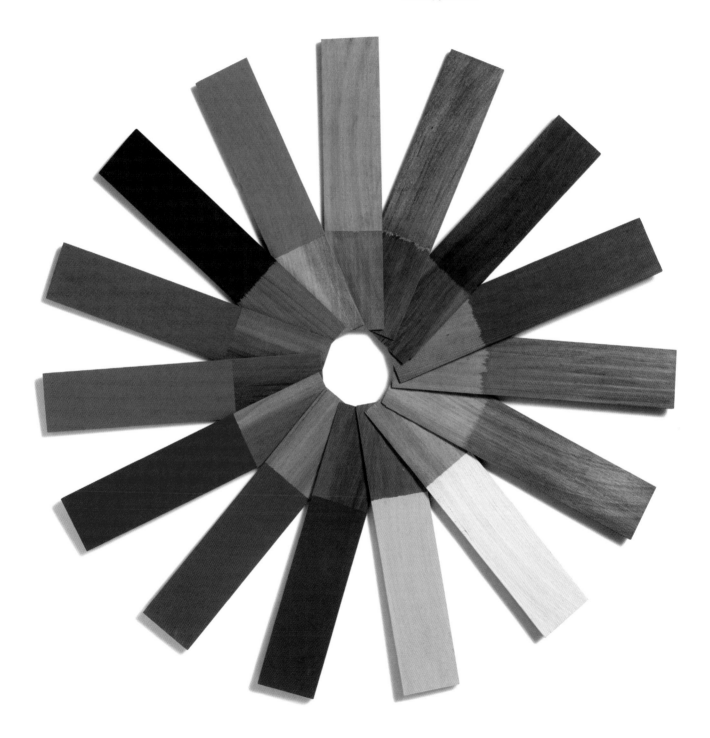

The Spectrum of Stain Color

Exterior stains fall into three basic categories: clear, semitransparent, and solid-color, depending on the percentage of solid pigments or resins present in the mixture. The less pigment in the stain, the more the wood grain shows through. Alternatively, the more pigment in the stain, the more opaque the color.

Clear/Transparent

Pros: • highlights the natural color of
         the wood
       • easy to apply, minimal lap marks
       • no film to peel
       • little preparation needed

Cons: • short-lived UV protection
       • frequent maintenance required
         to preserve "natural" wood color

Recoat: 1–2 years

Semitransparent

Pros: • moderate UV protection and
         durability
       • some color choice
       • highlights wood grain and
         texture
       • no film to peel

Cons: • obscures natural wood color
       • can show lap marks if brushed
         carelessly

Recoat: 3–5 years

Solid-Color

Pros: • best UV protection
       • most durable type of stain
       • wide color selections available
       • easy to apply
       • highlights wood texture

Cons: • hides wood color and grain
       • can peel (but not as readily as
         paint)

Recoat: 3–5 years for oils, 6–8 years for
        acrylics

RIGHT **This bold house combines a variety of colors, some of which are strikingly different, but all work in harmony.**

> **Tip: Check Batch Numbers**

To ensure all the stain you buy is the same color, check that the batch numbers on the cans are all the same. The numbers are usually on the tops or bottoms of the cans. When the numbers are the same, it means that the stain was manufactured and packaged at the same time, and color discrepancies from can to can are less likely. Even so, for best results, pour all the stain you are using into an empty five-gallon (19 liter) can and work from that.

Testing for Color

In looking for a particular stain color, at least when it comes to toners and semitransparent stains, any relationship between what is on the color chip in the brochure and how the material will look on the wood is—as I heard a painter say one day—"purely coincidental." Different woods absorb stains to different degrees, and even if you see the stain on a sample piece of wood in the store, it's not the wood that it's going on. Some people bring a sample piece of the wood that they are planning to stain, but this is imprecise as well. Stores commonly use fluorescent lighting, which distorts how the color appears, so you can't get an exact idea of what the wood will look like onsite. Of course, you may be able to bring the wood into the store and, assuming you are buying a standard rather than a custom color, have the can agitated, carefully apply a little, and take the sample back to the site to see how it looks.

Though it costs extra money in the short run, as was mentioned earlier, one way to ensure that you get the color you want is to buy stain in quarts and then apply it in an out-of-the-way spot, such as on the facing board of the deck, to see how it looks. You have to wait until the material dries—to dry it quickly, use a hair dryer—to get a true read on its color. Some companies provide small sample of stains, which makes it easier to determine which stain provides the color you want.

Color Inspiration for Stained Surfaces

Stain colors are available in hundreds of shades. Here are a few color palettes to illustrate the wide variety of colors that can be used together for a home.

Color Inspiration for Stained Surfaces

Color Inspiration for Stained Surfaces

Color Inspiration for Stained Surfaces

> Color Harmony

When you select stains for use on and around the house, make sure the colors of the stains harmonize with one another, even if you are using the stains on different surfaces. For example, if you use a brownish semitransparent stain on your cedar siding, you should use a compatible color on the trim, such as a white, light brown, or dark green. For ideas, look through manufacturers' booklets, check color ideas in this book, or just think it through yourself. Some other color tips follow:

- Colors must work together. On the exterior of a home, you are working with a number of colors—the roof, masonry materials such as brick or concrete, and landscaping. All should blend together, yet provide some contrast.

- A number of color experts subscribe to the idea of having three colors on the outside: one main color and two accent colors for the trim. In this scenario, the siding is one color, a little on the conservative side. The front door (as well as the rear door) and the windows are another color, which complements the siding color. The shutters, lamp post, mailbox, and house numbers can be another color. The colors, again, are different but complementary.

- In designing the color scheme, avoid using a color on the trim that is not complementary to the color of the siding. For example, a beige house with bright violet doors and windows and yellow shutters would look chaotic.

- Consider the direction the house faces when designing a color scheme. A house that faces east or west and has no shade may be too bright, calling for a cool color. On the other hand, a house that faces north and is in the shade may need a warm color.

- Do not draw attention to downspouts, gutters, electrical conduit, meters, air-conditioning units, and vents by painting them. If possible, these items should be the same color as the siding or trim so they are less noticeable.

- Do not draw attention to an attached garage by staining it a boldly different color. It should be the same color as the siding or a softer shade of it.

- For chimneys and foundations, use a deeper shade of the body color; doing so makes them seem more solidly mounted.

- Consider the color values used on a home and what they can do for it. Medium to dark colors usually make a house appear smaller, and light to neutral colors make it look strong.

- If you want to make a tall house seem shorter, coat the top a deeper tone than the bottom. This method also works when the lot on which the house sits is small and you want to reduce the visual size of the house, such as for new homes where the landscaping has not grown in and the house appears stark and overwhelming.

- Using a dark color to outline windows and trim makes a house look smaller. A lighter color on the trim makes a house look larger. In other words, dark outline colors tend to pull the size of a house in, whereas light ones expand it.

- Color ideas can come from a variety of places. Consider using a color you like from the inside of the home or pick up a color from exterior stonework or perhaps flowers or plants. You can also get color ideas from checking out the color schemes of similar-style homes in the neighborhood.

- Victorian and other period houses were painted specific colors. If you have a house of this type and want to know what the original colors were, check in the local library. At least one company (at this writing) produces a "Preservation Palette" color card, which shows the original colors of period houses.

- To test how combinations of colors work together, draw a picture of the home and shade various areas with colored pencils. Or take a photograph of the house then photocopy, enlarge, and color it. The colors are not necessarily accurate, but the image gives you the sense of how the colors will work.

> **Tip: Variations in Color and Tone**

Note that whenever you use a clear coating, toner, or semitransparent stain on wood—whether on a deck, siding, or anything else—the results will be somewhat uneven, with some parts a deeper color than others. Stain is not paint, in which the color is consistent throughout. Wood absorbs stain to varying degrees, even within a single piece, which accounts for the color variations. This mottled appearance is desirable. It is considered part of the natural beauty of a stained finish.

BELOW   **Stain can add colorful details around the home. Here, semi-solid stain was used on flower boxes to add a delightful touch.**

> Good Points to Remember

- Stain comes either in a penetrating or non-penetrating type. The former seeps into wood like sauce into a sponge cake whereas the latter forms a film. Paint also forms a film.

- Penetrating stains include clears, toners (which contain a little color) and semitransparents (which contain a lot of color). Solid-color stain is basically a flat paint that forms a film.

- Although paint lasts longer, it can peel. Penetrating stain does not peel unless it has been applied too heavily and allowed to dry into a film.

- Solid-color stain can peel but not as readily as paint.

- Solid-color stains that are meant to be walked on will likely wear out before they peel. They are also subject to mars from shoes.

- Some clear coatings are meant to protect against water intrusion only. Others protect against the graying effects of the sun and contain a preservative that protects against insects and fungi.

- Don't use varnish or polyurethane outdoors. It usually peels easily.

- If you like that silver gray look, apply weathering or bleaching oil.

- Apply a little of the stain to the backside of your wood to get a true read on its color.

- Because of environmental laws, VOCs, or volatile organic compounds, are limited in paint and stain and may lower their quality.

- When using a penetrating stain, always make sure it's going deeply into the wood. Backbrushing—going over wet stain with an undipped "dry" brush—usually ensures this.

- Always read the instructions on the can and follow them meticulously.

- Power washers make preparing surfaces for staining quicker.

> Tip: Best Performance

Penetrating stains perform best on rough sawn, weathered, or coarse-textured wood. If you are finishing smooth wood, power wash, sand, or wet the surface, then allow it to dry before finishing.

> Tip: Safety First

If you use oil-based stain, take care with the storage of applicators, particularly any rags or sponges. These items can combust spontaneously. If you discard such materials, your best bet is to seal them in an airtight container, immerse them in water in a container, or bury them.

ABOVE **This deck is coated with transparent stain. When you buy stain for a deck, make sure that it is formulated to stand up to foot traffic and the usual wear and tear of an outdoor surface.**

CHAPTER 2

Tools and Equipment

One of the keys to a good staining job is the quality of the tools and equipment you use. This chapter covers the various applicators, tools, and equipment, such as ladders, that you'll need for the typical staining job. Detailed information on each item is included so that you can make an informed choice. I also share some of my personal insights since it may help simplify the selection process for you.

In general, using quality tools and equipment will make for a better, safer, and easier job. A good brush will enable you to apply stain evenly and more efficiently than will a low quality brush. And the results will look better. A solid ladder will make you feel much more secure in those high-up places and you'll be able to better focus on your work. Knowing which type of sandpaper to use can also save you time and ensure a better job.

Of course, buying quality tools and materials may cost you a little more up front, but it will be a small amount in relation to the total job. Typically, the cost of materials such as stain or paint is fifteen percent of the job and labor is eighty-five percent. Buying brushes, rollers and equipment will cost just a few percent of the overall total—even if you're starting from scratch—and their cost will be spread over the many years, perhaps even decades—since quality materials can be used again and again, as long as you take care of them properly.

OPPOSITE **Quality tools can make or break the job. On this newly built home, a variety of wood surfaces have been treated with stain.**

A variety of tools and equipment is available to make staining easier and better. A roundup of these tools follows.

Applicators

Number one on the equipment hit parade, of course, are stain applicators. Numerous types are available, and, as you'll see, a variety can be used on the same surfaces, though some do have advantages over others in particular situations in terms of speed and ease of application.

Brushes

In general, the overall best applicator for most stains is the brush. It is good for clear coatings, semitransparent, and semi-solid stains—wherever you are applying stain to raw wood or wood that has been previously coated with a penetrable stain (with the exception of solid-color stain). You can also use a brush to apply a solid-color stain over a previous coating of solid-color stain or paint, though rollers and pads are faster.

Advantages of Brushes

The main advantage of a brush, as mentioned earlier, is that in using a brush, you can drive the stain more deeply into the wood pores, where it dries and locks in place.

The main thing to remember when selecting a brush—or any applicator, for that matter—is to buy high-quality equipment. Good brushes hold more stain and apply it more evenly and smoothly than a lower-quality brush. They also make the job look better, and they save a lot of time. It can take a painter twenty-five percent longer to paint with a low-quality brush than with a good one; a poor brush can make a job up to eighty percent longer. To translate that into real time, if a job took four hours with a good brush, it would take an extra three hours or so with a low-quality brush—and the job would not look as good. The same ratios also apply to staining. Another advantage is that certain parts of a job will likely involve "cutting in," staining areas that abut where you don't want the stain to go. Here, a brush is the only viable tool.

Most pros buy the best brushes and then take care of them, because they are the tools of their livelihood. Some painters have had brushes for decades.

BELOW Using the proper tool for the job can make a world of difference in the final results. A fluffy pad or brush will work well for this type of shingled siding.

of the paint being used was oil-based. The best of these brushes were made with bristles from Russian and Chinese hogs. The hogs, or wild boars, developed thick hair in response to harsh winters and the natural vegetation that nourished them. They were—and still are—the best natural bristles available today for several reasons.

First, hog bristles are long. The bristles wear down faster than synthetic bristles, but they still last a long time because of their length. Second, they are thinner and tapered at the ends, which tends to allow more control in applying the stain. Third, the ends are "flagged," or split. Flagged ends hold stain better and spread it more evenly than unsplit ends. Manufacturers of synthetic brushes have to manufacture flagged ends. If you are going to be working with oil-based products, I recommend using a natural-bristle brush. In general, synthetic brushes are designed for use with water-based products.

Synthetic Bristles

Brushes made with synthetic bristles are best used for water-based stain because they do not absorb much water. Nylon is one major synthetic material that absorbs only four percent of its own weight. Polyester, the other major synthetic material, does not absorb any water at all.

Although there is no question that synthetic materials should only be used for water-based stain, the question is, which of the synthetics is the best choice among them?

Pure nylon-bristle brushes are more flexible than polyester bristles and provide a smoother coat. They are also more abrasion-resistant and last longer than polyester bristles, particularly when used on a rough surface.

On the positive side for polyester, it holds its shape better when heat is intense. For example, at 100°F (38°C) nylon goes soft and polyester does not (though it makes one wonder who would be applying stain in such heat). Nylon is also sensitive to certain chemicals, such as ketones. Many synthetic bristles

There's no reason why the amateur can't do the same. Why work with a cheap brush, gum it up with stain, allow it to dry rock hard, and then toss it—requiring you to get a new brush next time you stain?

Natural Bristles

When buying a brush, consider a number of aspects of the brush. A major element of a brush is the bristles. Two kinds of bristle are available: animal hair, which are natural animal hairs, and synthetic, or man-made bristles. A cardinal rule in staining (and painting) is that natural or animal-hair brushes (also called China bristle because of their origin) must be used with oil-based stain. If they are used with water-based stain the natural hollowness of the bristles absorbs moisture—up to forty percent of their weight. Hence, they swell and become soft and limp, just as human hair does when wet—not very good for applying stain.

Prior to World War II, all brushes were made of animal hair rather than synthetic materials. Indeed, synthetic materials were not needed because most

BELOW **Large ceilings and porch floors, such as the one shown here, can be stained more efficiently by starting with a roller and finishing with a brush to backbrush the material into the surface.**

are blends of nylon and polyester, with the idea being to combine the best qualities of each type of material while keeping the negative characteristics out. This type of synthetic-bristle brush would be my choice.

Bristle ends can be either square cut, tapered, or chisel cut (also called chisel-edged), in which the bristles on the inside of the brush are longer than those on the outside. The tapered brushes allow you to make a sharper line, facilitating cutting in. With flat or non-tapered brushes, all the bristles are the same

length. Such brushes are used when precision is wanted but for doing broad, flat areas. The angled brushes make it easier to stain windows in particular; their bristles are cut so that they do not suffer stress when paint is applied and, thus, last longer.

Construction

A high-quality brush is well made. For one thing, the butt ends of the bristles are firmly anchored inside the ferrule—the metal band that goes around the brush

OPPOSITE **On large expanses, a roller can save time for the preliminary application by quickly getting the stain on. Step two is to backbrush the stain to work it thoroughly into the surface. A brush is the best tool to use on this vertical siding, as it makes it easier to control a penetrating stain's application.**

BELOW **A quality roller showing a sleeve with a $\frac{3}{4}$" (1.9 cm) nap, which many painters like for applying solid-color stains. Note the formed handle and cage-type assembly, which makes it easier to take the sleeve on and off. Also, the sleeve is made of phenolic-impregnated kraft paper.**

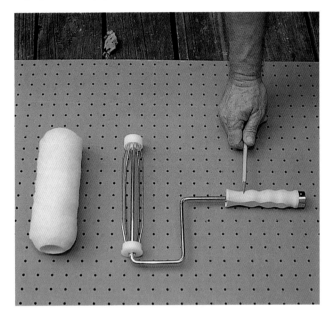

and holds the bristle assembly to the handle. The bristles may be attached by vulcanized rubber or an epoxy glue that is resistant to water, oil, and solvents. Such brushes do not shed their bristles. The ferrule may be made of stainless steel, nickel, or brass.

High-quality brushes also have plugs inside the ferrule made of wood, aluminum, plastic, or a specially treated cardboard. First, the plugs ensure a tight bond of the bristles in the ferrule. Second, they add taper to the brush, making it thicker at the base of the bristles and narrower at the ends, allowing for a sharper line. Third, they provide wells inside the bristles, which allows more paint to be loaded without dripping and keeps the center of the brush somewhat open for easier cleaning. Some brushes also have an insert—a narrow metal band inside the ferrule.

Handles

Handles are made of plastic or wood. Wood tends not to slip out of one's grasp whereas plastic does. However, wood can crack and split if it is left in cleaning solutions for prolonged periods. The handle should counterbalance the weight of the bristles. Handles come in various shapes—try them out, much as you would try on a pair of shoes, before purchasing.

Quality Testing

You can test a brush for quality. Every new brush sheds a few bristles. But when you fan the bristles a few times and they continue to fall out, the brush's quality is suspect. When pressed against a surface, the bristles should bend one-third to one-half in relation to the tips. Also, when pressed against a dry surface, the bristles should not divide into clumps, or "finger." If they do, they will also finger when wet, and an uneven application will result. Finally, the bristles should snap back into position after this dry bending.

Sizes

Brushes come in various sizes: 1" (2.5 cm), 1½" (3.8 cm), 2" (5.1 cm), 3" (7.6 cm), 4" (10.2 cm), and 5" (12.5 cm). Just what sizes you select is more or less arbitrary, within reason. You can count on a 2" (5.1 cm) angled brush for trim, such as windows, a 3" (7.6 cm) brush for wider areas, and a 4" (10.2 cm) or 5" (12.5 cm) brush for broad siding, such as clapboard.

The round brush, also potentially useful, has bristles arranged in a circle. When the brush is applied to a surface, such as a railing, it tends to wrap itself around the surface. (Its bristle design also prevents it from fingering.) Another useful brush is the staining brush. This brush is 5" (12.5 cm) wide and thick and has many fine bristles. The bristles are fine because stain is much thinner than paint. This brush has a removable handle—you can screw a long handle into the brush to use it like a broom to coat a deck.

> **Tip: Buy Quality**
> Your best bet for a buying a brush is to buy high quality and take care of it. It may cost more to begin with, but it is far cheaper in the long run.

Rollers

You will use rollers less when applying penetrating stains (clears, toners, semitransparent) than when applying solid-color stains. Rollers can't drive these products into the wood surface—which, of course, you want to do with stains—as other applicators do. Rollers are good applicators for solid-color stain, because its application is essentially like that of paint. However, on big jobs you can use rollers with penetrating stain. The rollers do a quick job of getting the stain on the surface. Then, to drive it into the wood pores, use a brush to "backbrush" it—go over it with a dry brush.

The standard roller is 9" (22.9 cm), though they can be found longer (up to 18" [45.7 cm]) and shorter (6" [15.2 cm] and 7" [17.8 cm]). For staining, the 9" (22.9 cm) size serves well. You can also try some smaller-size rollers, 3" (7.6 cm) and 4" (10.2 cm), that are useful when applying stain to narrow areas.

The pile or nap—the material that covers the roller sleeve—is made of various materials and thicknesses, from $\frac{3}{16}$" (0.5 cm), $\frac{3}{8}$" (1 cm), $\frac{3}{4}$" (1.9 cm), up to $1\frac{1}{2}$" (3.8 cm). For applying clear coating and semi-transparent stain to rough surfaces, the thicker-nap rollers are useful. They can carry more stain to the rugged surface, and when you roll the stain on, it slops into the various surface grooves and fissures and then can be backbrushed. You can use any roller

BELOW **This location will greatly benefit from stain protection. Salty air and water will assault it.**

length for applying solid-color stain; the shorter-nap rollers are effective because they lay on a paint-like film. On smooth surfaces, I suggest you use the standard $\frac{3}{8}$"- (1 cm) or $\frac{1}{2}$"- (1.3 cm) thick nap. If you are applying concrete stain to concrete, either a $\frac{3}{8}$" (1 cm) or $\frac{1}{4}$" (0.6 cm) nap should be used, depending on roughness.

> Tip: What Painters Like

Some painters like to use a $\frac{3}{4}$"- (1.9 cm) nap roller to apply solid-color stain. Although it applies a lot of stain, by the time it comes to smoothing out the stain, it will have flatted out to a film that is the equivalent of having applied it with a $\frac{1}{2}$" (1.3 cm) roller.

Roller-Fabric Types

As with brush bristles, the fabric that naps are made of may be natural—lamb's wool—or synthetic—Dacron, nylon, polyester, or orlon.

The natural-fabric naps should not be used with water-based stain because the water makes the fibers swell and go limp. You can usually use synthetic fibers with oil-based solvents, but because some of them contain very strong solvents, it best to read the roller label to see if they are allowed.

The Sleeve

Another quality consideration is the type of core, or sleeve, to which the fabric is attached. Poor-quality sleeves can come apart and are usually indicative of a poor-quality nap.

Roller sleeves are made of plastic, phenolic-impregnated kraft paper, or cardboard. The phenolic sleeves are best because they are not affected by constantly being dipped in a liquid; they keep their shape indefinitely. Plastic sleeves are good, but they can soften when exposed to certain solvents. The lowest-quality sleeves are made of cardboard. These come apart quite quickly and should be avoided. If you can see seams through the nap, reject the sleeve. Those seams not only indicate poor quality but also can leave marks on the surface. Also, squeeze the roller and release. Does it pop back into shape or does it keep its squeezed shape? If it does not regain its shape when it is dry, it certainly will not do so when soaked with paint.

> Good Points to Remember

- The best applicator for a penetrating stain is usually a brush, because it can drive the product into the wood pores. Rollers also work well, particularly on rough surfaces, which soak up penetrating stains.

- Solid-color stain can be applied with the same applicators (brush, roller, or pad) that you use with paint.

- Spraying stain is a good way to go if you are coating large areas, such as a house. The airless type of sprayer is fastest.

- Pads work very well for applying penetrating and solid-color stains.

- For staining—or painting—it's best to buy the best-quality tools you can and then take care of them.

- Hook-type scrapers are good for removing peeling stain or paint.

- Sandpaper in a sanding block works better than just folding it over.

- The HVLP sprayer is good for fine work but is not powerful enough to do entire rooms or houses.

Roller Handles

Rollers handles—the part you grip and slip the roller onto—come in a variety of qualities and sizes. The standard size, like the roller, is 9" (22.9 cm).

The handle may be made of plastic or wood. Wood handles are usually an indication of high quality. One advantage of wood handles is that excess stain is absorbed into the wood; this does not happen with a plastic handle. Better-quality wood and plastic handles are configured for gripping. Poorer-quality handles are not usually shaped for gripping.

ABOVE **A stain job that is done right will last years without peeling or weather damage, even in areas where natural elements are harsh.**

Roller handles, which are also known as roller frames, are available in three types of construction: a solid cylinder, which can be made of metal or plastic; an open style with floating end caps; and a spring-cage frame with four or five thick wires. This last type allows you to slip roller sleeves on and off more easily.

Just as you can backbrush with a brush, when you use a roller, you may able to just "backroll." Apply the stain to small areas as suggested in various chapters for various surfaces, and then use an unloaded or dry roller to even out the stain. If the stain doesn't appear to be driven into the wood, then use a brush to do so.

> **Tip: Rule of Thumb**

The rule of thumb is: the rougher the surface, the thicker the nap should be.

> Tip: Excess Stain on Surfaces

Never leave excess stain on a surface. As will be detailed later, you should carefully follow the manufacturer's recommendation on application rates. Excess stain may not penetrate the wood and will dry into a film, which may then peel.

Trays

Roller trays are made of either plastic or metal and are commonly of a width to accommodate a 9"- (22.9 cm) wide roller. One main consideration in buying a tray is to get one deep enough to hold the paint well. Shallow trays do not hold a lot of stain—frequent refilling is required and it is likely that paint will slop over the edges.

Thin, plastic tray liners are available, but it is not a good idea to use them. They are too shallow; when placed in a deep tray, they make the tray, in effect, shallow, too. (In a pinch a tray can be lined with heavy-duty—not light-duty—aluminum foil.)

Plastic trays may be made of thin to fairly thick plastic. Thin plastic is not good because it is bendable, which can be a real liability when you must move a tray that is half-filled with stain from one spot to another without spilling.

Trays may have ladder-lock feet on them to enable you to lock the tray securely onto a stepladder.

Pads

Pads come in various sizes and with various naps, from smooth to fluffy. The smooth pad is normally narrow enough to slip under shingles whose butts or bottoms are slightly raised. Thus, you can apply the stain in one sweep, rather than cutting in the butts with a brush.

Pads for Decks

As mentioned earlier, the best way to apply stains or clear finishes to a deck is usually by brush, because the pressure created by the brushstrokes works the stain

ABOVE **This fluffy pad attached to a threaded pole does a good job applying any kind of stain, allowing you to apply and backbrush material into wood.**

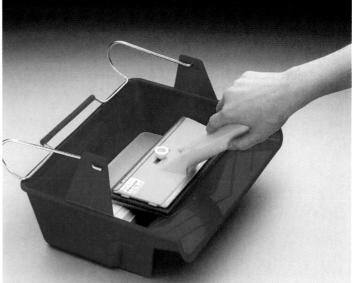

ABOVE **A flat pad can be loaded with stain by passing it across ridged roller. The pad allows you to apply stain in a wiping motion, and its narrow edges can catch under shingle courses.**

into the wood. However, the pad is the second-best applicator; some would say it's as good as a brush.

Most pads, like roller handles, can accept threaded poles, although these are usually force-fit—there are no threads. The pole allows you to apply the stain from a standing position rather than have to bend over, as brush application requires. You can also use a 5" (12.5 cm) staining brush with a pole screwed into it and apply the stain in a broomlike fashion. (The original manufacturer of pads is Padco, and they make an excellent product. Today there are many other manufacturers, but they vary in quality so be sure to choose a sturdy one of good quality.)

Paint Sprayers

Paint sprayers can also be used for applying stain. Indeed, spraying stain can be a boon for the do-it-yourselfer as well as the pro because it makes the job go more quickly. Spray-staining a surface can be twice as fast as applying the stain with a roller. Spraying started out as a tool in the industry for painting irregular shapes and items, but because of its speed in some situations, its use has spread to both the inside and outside of houses.

Types of Sprayers

Three kinds of sprayers are available: conventional, high-volume low-pressure (HVLP), and airless.

Conventional Sprayers

All types use air to atomize the stain, but the conventional system, also called the cup-and-gun system, atomizes it into a very fine mist and expels it from the spray gun by using compressed air. In airless systems, a pump is used, and the coating droplets are much heavier. With the airless sprayer, most often used by painters, there is little overspray, so it can be used

BELOW **Spraying is a good method when the areas to be stained are large. You must first cover anything that could be hit by overspray.**

OPPOSITE **Professionals use spray techniques to saturate large areas more quickly such as on the house. But remember, stain still needs to be backbrushed.**

RIGHT **Time consuming but necessary, a previously painted surface must be scraped to prepare for a new coat of solid-color stain. This sage green door shows the benefits of proper preparation.**

inside. This feature is important. If you are spraying near a neighbor's house, you want to make sure overspray is limited or guarded against with drop cloths or moving objects out of harm's way. You don't want a cloud of semitransparent stain settling on your neighbor's car. Each system works only on certain materials. The thicker the material in the conventional system, the more it must be thinned.

HVLP Sprayers

The high-volume low-pressure sprayer is the newest kind of spray equipment available. It looks like a conventional cup-and-gun sprayer, but the significant difference is that the HVLP sprayer requires only ten pounds of pressure to operate, as opposed to eighty to 130 pounds that the conventions sprayer requires.

This difference allows far greater control of the spray. The HVLP sprayer is good for fine work but is not powerful enough to do large areas, such as rooms or houses.

Airless Sprayers

Airless sprayers do not atomize the spray in the same way that cup-and-gun types do; airless sprayers also do not require that the paint be atomized to work well. They are airless. They depend on pressure—from 1,200 to 3,000 pounds—to drive the stain through a nozzle where the stain is broken up into particle size and delivered as a thick, airless, wet film where ever you want it. Unlike conventional sprayers, a guard is not required when spraying, meaning an experienced painter can paint close to other areas without shielding them or masking them off. In some instances, spray guards, which are about 36" (91.4 cm) long and 12" (30.5 cm) wide, are useful. They are made of plastic or metal with a handle and resemble a huge fan.

Airless sprayers are faster than conventional guns. A good airless sprayer can apply one gallon (3.8 liter) of stain in three minutes. Usually, painters work out of a five-gallon (19 liter) container; the stain is drawn up into the spray gun via a hose.

Another plus of an airless sprayer is its transfer efficiency—the amount of stain that is actually transferred from the sprayer to the surface and that is not oversprayed or wasted.

> **Tip: Great Caution**
>
> Great caution is necessary with an airless spray gun. Because of the tremendous pressures it generates, it can cut through flesh with ease.

Drop Cloths

I once knew a painter who was so good and so neat that he did not require drop cloths. I must say that the sight of him painting in a living room containing wall-to-wall carpeting, glass-top tables, and the like without protecting them was very unusual. Most of us, however, are mere mortals, and we do need to use drop cloths outside as well as inside. A variety are available, some of which are waterproof (or paint- and stainproof), whereas others are not.

Plastic drop cloths come in various thicknesses and sizes, usually ranging from $\frac{1}{25}$" (1 mm) to $\frac{1}{5}$" (6 mm) thick. As the sheeting gets thicker, the overall size gets bigger. Hence, a 9' x 12' (2.7 m x 3.7 m) plastic drop cloth might be $\frac{1}{5}$" (1 mm) or $\frac{2}{25}$" (2 mm) thick whereas a 10' x 20' (3 m x 6.1 m) one might be $\frac{1}{5}$" (4 mm) thick. I would suggest that you use the $\frac{1}{5}$" (1 mm) or $\frac{2}{25}$" (2 mm) size. With these, the plastic is thick enough that the slightest breeze won't make it float in the air.

Canvas drop cloths also work well. They come in various weights. The 8-ounce (226.8-gram) size, while not leakproof, usually does the job fine.

For a neater, cleaner, quicker job, always cover all areas that you don't want to get stain on before you begin. It's faster than stopping and moving drop cloths every time you move to a new area.

Scrapers

If you are applying solid-color stain to a previously painted or solid-color-stained surface, some removal of paint may be required. For this job, a variety of scrapers are available. The classic kind is the straight-blade scraper, which looks like a putty knife but has a larger blade. I recommend the one with the $3\frac{1}{2}$" (8.9 cm) blade, which is available as both a flexible and rigid blade. For scraping, the rigid blade works best. If you expect to do some patching of holes, get the kind with the flexible blade. It smoothes out patches more easily.

Hook-Type Scraper

If you have to remove a lot of peeling paint, a hook-type scraper works best. These are available in a few sizes but essentially consist of a long handle with a blade on the end. This blade is a flat piece of metal with two edges sharpened and bent over. Pull the

> **Dealing with Power Lines**
>
> If you're afraid of contacting power lines while working outside, note that some power companies, if given enough notice, will disconnect incoming power lines where they connect with trim so the do-it-yourselfer has free access to work without any risk of shock. The power company normally provides alternate power so the occupants' lives are not disrupted while the regular power line is down.

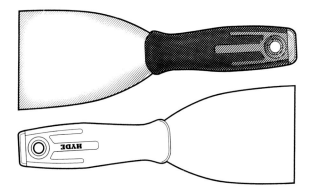

ABOVE **Scrapers are the standard tools for removing peeling paint. Some have flexible blades and some rigid. Rigid blades work best on peeling paint.**

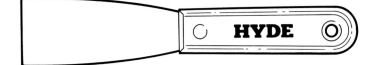

ABOVE **A putty knife comes in handy for applying glazing compound to windows. It also can be used as a scraper.**

ABOVE **Hook-type scrapers are good when you must deal with large areas of peeling paint. The blade can be rotated to provide a new edge.**

hook across the area where paint is peeling. Its big asset is the pressure with which it can be applied. When one edge of the blade wears down, a new edge can be used. Loosen the screw holding the blade to the handle and then rotate the blade to bring the new edge into play. Even better, you can get the hook-type scraper with a carbon-steel blade that you can sharpened with a file.

Razor Blade Scraper

Occasionally, during painting or staining, some of the material takes an errant path to glass. If it dries by the time you want to clean it up, your best bet is a razor blade scraper. The tool uses ordinary single-edge razor blades, which you can retract by pushing a button back or forth.

Putty Knives

A putty knife, so called because its main job is to apply window putty, or glazing compound, are also essential. These tools come with plastic or wooden handles.

Sandpaper

Any rough edges left by scraping should be smoothed with sandpaper. Sandpaper is essentially an abrasive material bonded to a backing of paper or other material. It is classified by the type of abrasive or grit used, its weight, type of coating, and grit number. The back of the sandpaper describes what type of grit is available and the degree of fineness.

Four grit materials are commonly used: aluminum oxide, emery, garnet, and silicon carbide. The grits come in various degrees of hardness and are suitable for sanding different materials. Garnet, a reddish brown abrasive, is the softest of all and is used on wood almost exclusively. Emery, a black abrasive, is used on metal. Next up the scale of hardness is aluminum oxide, a reddish abrasive that is exceptionally hard and long-wearing and can be used on wood, painted surfaces, alloy steel, high-carbon steel, tough bronzes, and some hardwoods. The hardest grit of all is silicon carbide, a bluish black sandpaper that is good on metals and needn't play a role in wood sanding. I would suggest that the best kind to get is aluminum oxide, the reddish sandpaper.

Grits come in varying degrees of coarseness, varying from 12—which is very coarse—to 1200—which is superfine. (The higher the grit number, the smoother the material.) If you are using a sanding machine, use lower numbers than those used for hand sanding.

Sandpaper also comes in open- and closed-coated varieties. On closed-coated papers the grit particles cover all the paper, which leads to the paper becoming clogged with the material being sanded. Open-coated papers have more space between grit particles and do not clog as quickly. Indeed, they can be cleaned and reused.

To smooth a scraped area, fold over a sheet of sandpaper and sand where needed. A number of accessories are available that can make working with the material easier. One tool is a sanding block. For a standard sanding block, cut the paper to the proper length, then clamp the ends in place on a rubber sanding surface.

> **Tip: Saving Money**

    If you expect to do a lot of sanding with a sanding block, you can save money by cutting standard sandpaper sheets into block-sized pieces rather than buying them precut, which, like prepared food, costs more than if you do it yourself.

Sometimes, you may have to sand something high, like a porch ceiling. Here, a sanding stick is handy. It accepts paper as other blocks do, but the blocks are made so they swivel when screwed into the stick and allow the surface of the block to stay in 100 percent contact with the surface being sanded. Such blocks are made of plastic and metal; the metal one is better.

Ladders

Anyone staining the exterior of a house also must have access to a couple kinds of ladders. The two kinds commonly used are the stepladder and the extension ladder.

Stepladders

As with any other equipment, buy a high-quality stepladder. They come in three grades: type 3, or household grade; type 2, or commercial grade; and type I, industrial grade. Type 1 is rated at 200 pounds, type 2 at 225 pounds, and type 3 at 250 pounds, but the weight tests are conducted at four times these values.

If possible, get the type 1 ladder. The standard length is 6' (1.8 m), but they are available in lengths from 2" (61 cm) to 16' (4.9 m). A 6' (1.8 m) ladder is usually best. Ladders are made of wood, metal, or fiberglass. Fiberglass and wood are heavy whereas

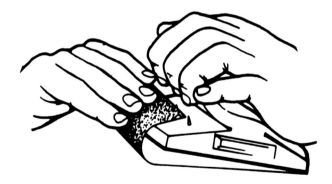

ABOVE **A piece of sandpaper is placed over the rubber face of the sanding block and the ends clamped in place on top of device. Using a sanding block gives you better control when sanding.**

>Ladders and Safety

Every year, hundreds of people are killed or injured while using ladders. Improper use of a ladder also results in less efficiency. Ladder safety is partly a function of using a good-quality ladder, but you should also consider the following safety procedures:

• Inspect ladders on a daily basis. This is an exercise not in advanced science but in common sense. Are rails split or broken? Is something bent? Are bolts loose? If you have any questions about the equipment being totally safe, do not use it. If a ladder cannot be repaired (and good-quality ladders can be), discard it—but first destroy it by running over it with a truck or cutting it up. You do not want someone at the dump to pick up such a ladder and use it.

• When you are using the ladder, do not stretch. Stain or paint only what you can easily see and reach. This may mean moving a heavy extension ladder more often than you would like, but the alternative is to take a chance of falling. Of course, some stretching is required from time to time, but do not put yourself in jeopardy.

• Do not "jump" the ladder—move the top of it to reach a missed spot—from one position to another while you are standing on it.

• Get help if you cannot move or manage a large ladder alone. A toppling ladder can cause serious damage to people and property.

• Do not make the ladder lean too much or too little. The rule when you are leaning an extension ladder against a house is that the bottom should be one quarter of the ladder height away from the house. Sometimes bushes and other obstructions interfere with this theory, but adhere to it as much as possible. If the ladder is set too steeply against a wall, it could topple backward; if it is positioned too far from the wall, the front end could slide down the siding.

• Make sure the legs cannot slide out. Do not set the legs of the ladder in soft earth. Sometimes you can solve the problem of soft earth by banging homemade pegs into the ground in front of the ladder's feet. If the ground is not soft, put some sort of weight there —a pair of concrete blocks— or, if necessary, tie the legs in place in some fashion.

• Make sure the ladder cannot fall sideways. This can be a problem when you are staining a house on rough terrain. The legs may not be on exactly level terrain, and a shift in weight can send it toppling. To level the legs, use C clamps to add a board to the foot of the shorter leg to lengthen it and make it level with the other. Commercial extensions are also available.

• Do not stand on the top step of the ladder to reach something. Get a taller ladder.

• Do not work on a ladder in front of an unlocked door— this is an accident waiting to happen. Neither the board nor the painter should ever go on top of the ladder. Someone could come out, the door smacks into the ladder, and down you go.

• Do not work outside when there's a strong wind or a lightning storm.

• The best procedure when you set up a ladder is to climb up on it a few steps and see if it is stable before you climb higher.

• If you are using an aluminum or wooden ladder, by all means be careful that you are not in danger of tipping or falling into an electrical line. If the line is frayed, the shock could easily kill you.

ABOVE **Regular extension ladders can be used to stain this house. Extend the ladder from the ground up flat to the angle of the roof, parallel to the dormer. While working on the ladder, have someone foot the ladder on solid ground.**

metal weighs perhaps half of what wood does. Although it is sturdy, aluminum can bend a little, which might seem disconcerting. The best bet is to climb up the ladder in the store and see how you like each kind.

Extension Ladders

Extension ladders are available in sizes up to 40' (12.2 m) and, like stepladders, are made of wood, aluminum, or fiberglass. Aluminum is the lightest, but it does conduct electricity. Wood is heavy and can also conduct electricity when wet. Fiberglass is not conductive. Many professional painters prefer fiberglass ladders for the simple reason that they do not conduct electricity.

Extension ladders come in various grades. Type 1 is the strongest grade available. It does not necessarily mean, however, that the ladder is top-quality. Here, stick to good brands, and get their top-of-the-line product. An extension ladder that accepts replacement parts is an indication of top quality.

are coating windows. It lets you coat the entire window from one ladder position—directly in front of it.

Roof brackets are also handy. Here, shingles are lifted, and the brackets are secured beneath with nails driven into the decking. A board is then extended across them, providing a scaffold off of which to work. This setup is excellent for safe and easier staining of dormers.

> Tip: Securing Roof Brackets

Only secure the brackets in the morning when roof shingles are not soft. If you lift them when soft, say, after a day in sunlight, they could tear. Some painters wet them down to cool them off before lifting them.

Miscellaneous Equipment

Various other tools can be useful when planning and executing a staining project.

Utility Knife

A utility knife is a useful tool. A variety of types are sold, but the standard consists of a handle in which blades are mounted with more or less of the cutting edge exposed by manipulation of a button, which slides the blade forward or backward.

Wire Brushes

If you're working with solid stain and have to take peeling paint off surfaces, a wire brush can be useful. They are particularly helpful where the surface is ridged, such as striated siding, which does not readily allow you to use a standard scraper. Here, just pull the wire brush along the ridged surface. Its stiff yet flexible wires do a good job of removing peeling paint.

Wire brushes come in a variety of configurations, from those shaped like scrub brushes to ones with long, curved handles to ones with wide handles. Pick one that looks like an enlarged toothbrush. Wire brush bristles are made of a variety of materials.

ABOVE **The varying levels of this property require more than one type of ladder to insure a safe and efficient site for the worker.**

Ladder Accessories

Many ladder accessories are available, but by far the most common and popular are ladder jacks, which hook onto rungs and across which an extension plank—or just a stout board—can be laid. These jacks come in various versions but are inexpensive and efficient. They can also be rented.

A "standoff" accessory that hooks onto the top of the ladder can also be useful, particularly when you

Stainless steel is recommended. The other types—steel, aluminum, and brass—wear away while in use and can leave a metallic residue on the surface, which can change the surface texture and mar the job by reflecting sun improperly.

Tack Cloth

After wood is sanded, a certain amount of dust is left, and it is important to remove this. If an oil-based product is going to be applied, use the tack cloth to wipe up the dust. The small square of cloth is sticky and is designed to take off more dust than mere dusting would accomplish.

If a water-based product is to be used, then a damp cloth is advisable. The tack cloth leaves a residue that can interfere with water-based coating adhesion.

Other Equipment

• Electric Drill—A drill is required for a variety of jobs. Equipped with the right accessory, it can be used to strip paint or stain. You can also use a mixing bit to mix stain. Electric drills are available in corded and cordless models.

• Nail Set—Many times in staining siding, the do-it-yourselfer discovers that nail heads are protruding slightly. For a neater job, you should set the nails at the proper depth, something the nail set achieves quite well.

• Spinner Tool—This tool for good for cleaning brushes and rollers. Mount the brush or roller on the spinner, and pump the handle, much as you would use an eggbeater. The brush or roller spins rapidly, driving off excess stain and solvent. It is best to do this inside a large box so that overspray does not stain nearby objects. This tool is also known as a dry spinner.

> **Tip: Good Trick**
> A good way to shake excess stain or paint from of a brush is to put it in a bag, except for the handler. Holding the mouth of the bag tightly against the handle, grasp the handle and shake the material out.

BELOW **The spinner tool is great for getting stain or paint off a brush (left) or roller (right) before washing it.**

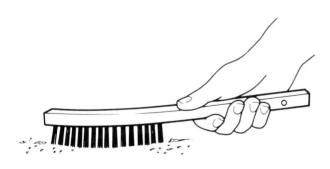

ABOVE **If you have to scrape paint or foreign matter from a ridged surface, the wire brush comes in handy for getting in the grooves. Don't leave loose metal bristles on the surface, however. Wipe them off, because they can interact with stain and cause unsightly iron stains.**

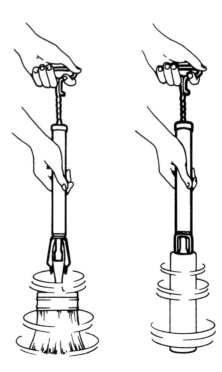

ABOVE **Here, a roller could be used to apply stain. A round brush would work well on the columns and a fluffy pad could be used on the ceiling.**

- Brush Extender—Sometimes you may have to apply stain in a location that is difficult to reach, despite the fact that you have a ladder. Invaluable here is an accessory that I call a brush extender, which consists of a threaded device that can be screwed onto a pole. The brush is then clamped into the device, allowing the pole and brush to become an extension, or brush extender, of your hand.

- Safety Glasses—Many types are available, in plastic as well as hardened, shatterproof glass, in plain and prescription lenses. You should wear glasses when you are power washing, chipping, or sanding because debris can fly off a surface, right into your eyes.

- Goggles—These are large glasses with protective sidepieces. They are used mainly for protection against the errant splash of harmful chemicals, but some types are made to withstand impacts, which are unlikely to occur while doing exterior staining.

- Breathing Masks—A number of products on the market protect, to varying degree, against harmful vapors and dust. Before you purchase any breathing apparatus, make sure it is adequate for the task at hand. Any mask must fit tightly. An ill-fitting mask can leak and be dangerous, offering only the illusion of protection.

  If you are doing a lot of sanding and want to protect against breathing dust, use the standard painter's mask—a cone-shaped, white paper mask with a rubber band to affix it to your face. It protects against dust but not vapors.

- Power Washers—Also called pressure washers, these tools deliver a high-pressure stream of water that—depending on the pounds per square inch, or psi, used—can be used for everything from cleaning a car to driving paint off wood. Essentially, water from your garden hose is run through the machine, which raises it to a certain pressure and drives it out of a spray wand. The greater the pressure, the tougher the jobs a power washer can do—literally everything from driving soil off wood to driving paint off.

Power washers, which can be bought or rented, come in both gas and electric versions. A key consideration is the psi the machine is capable of generating—the higher the number the greater the pressure. Generally, gas machines are capable of 1,300 to 2,400 psi, whereas electric machines deliver about 1,300 to 1,400. Electric machines are considered light duty, usually cost less than $200, and are used for such jobs as washing cars, garage floors, and outdoor patios. They are light and easier to move around than gas-powered units. Of course, in using them, be particularly wary of electrical shock. They require 12- or 14-gauge extension cords and must be plugged into a ground fault circuit interrupter, or GFCI.

The majority of power washers for sale or rent are the gas-powered kind. In general, they require more water—two to three gallons (7.6 to 11.4 liters) per minute, or gpm. To bring new life to a deck, siding, or fence, gas-powered washers should be the only choice. These machine cost anywhere from $330 to $850, with the cost relating to the power the machine is capable of as well as the features it has, such as chemical injectors and the pump and engine quality.

ABOVE **A power washer in action. It makes quick, thorough work of wood-cleaning jobs, but pressure and closeness to wood should be observed so wood is not accidentally scored.**

LEFT **This type of mask is good for protection against dust. To guard against vapors, you must get a mask made specifically for that task.**

CHAPTER 3

Preparation

This chapter illustrates how much easier it is to prepare wood for staining than it is for painting. If you are applying a penetrating stain to new wood, all you have to do is make sure the wood is clean. If you are applying a solid-color stain, which forms a film, priming is usually recommended so it may take a little more time. However once you've prepared the wood for the first time, when it comes time to restain, it's even simpler: All you have to do is make sure that the wood is clean again, which will normally take just as hour or two, even for an entire house.

In comparison, if you are preparing to repaint a surface, chances are you will have to scrape off peeling paint, fill cracks, perhaps add another coat of primer. It's not an exaggeration to predict that to prepare the average house properly for painting will take two or three days and sometimes much longer. This is one of the major advantages of using stain over paint.

It's not a good idea to take shortcuts when preparing a surface, because there is a direct relationship between the longevity of a job and how the surface is prepared. If you leave mildew on the wood, it will eat its way through and become a flaw on the new surface. So take care and do a thorough job. Read on for all the details.

OPPOSITE **Even a mountain hideaway in a damp, cool area can be protected from the potential ravages of moisture when given a first-class stain treatment with a quality product.**

Preparing a surface for staining—anything from a deck to siding—can be crucial in terms of how the final job turns out. Wood can be damaged or marred in a variety of ways, and it's a good idea to understand what you're up against and how to deal with it before you begin. The wood may be brand new or may have been previously coated. We will address both scenarios.

Ability to Absorb

If you intend to use a penetrating stain, you should first check to see how well the stain penetrates the surface. Sprinkle some water on the wood to be coated in various places. If the water beads up or otherwise looks like it's not being absorbed, the stain will not be absorbed either. A finish or something called mill glaze may be on the wood, which blocks absorption. To get the wood to accept the stain, you must strip it to expose the bare wood. (For more on stripping, see chapter four, page 80.)

Loose Fibers and Peeling

Sometimes the wood on the surface is "friable"—wood fibers are lying loosely on it, which is something that the sun may have caused. If these fibers are not removed the new coating won't adhere. To test for loose fibers, as well as loose finish, adhere a few adhesive bandages on the wood, and then pull them off rapidly. Examine the adhesive portions of the bandages. If any finish or debris is sticking to them, the finish must be stripped and/or the fibers removed.

ABOVE **To test a wood's absorbency for stain, sprinkle a little water on the wood. If within fifteen minutes it is absorbed, as shown on the left but not the right, the wood is ready to be stained.**

ABOVE **Before staining a deck, perform the adhesive bandage test. After cleaning the wood, adhere a few bandages to the wood and pull them off quickly to see if they pick up debris or peeling finish. If so, the debris or finish must be removed before you apply the stain.**

Preparing Bare Wood

Mill Glaze

Mill glaze is a problem that usually shows up on smooth, flat-grained western red cedar siding, and occasionally on other wood species, such as redwood. Although there is controversy over what causes it, it seems to be the result of using dull planer blades at the mill and is heightened by the difficult-to-plane flat-grained surface of the lumber. Nevertheless, the result is that water-soluble extractives are brought to the surface of the wood and create a hard, varnish like glaze. As these extractives age, particularly in direct sunlight, they become insoluble and difficult to remove. If the glaze occurs prior to final planning, the last step usually removes it.

Whatever the reason, mill glaze may not be penetrated by stain or clear coatings and must be dealt with. The easiest way to determine if your wood has mill glaze is to sprinkle some water on a couple spots. If the water does not penetrate, then you know it's mill glaze. Sanding the wood lightly with #80 sandpaper breaks the glaze and solves the problem.

Mildew

As mentioned earlier in the book, mildew is a fungus that grows on wood. Although it doesn't do any structural damage to the wood, it is unsightly and shows through clear coatings or toner stains. It is also an indication that conditions are ripe for rot, which can do serious damage to wood. Mildew is normally seen as clusters of gray or black dots or patches, but it can also appear green, red, and even yellow. Mildew needs moisture to grow, so you may find it on certain areas of the house that aren't getting enough sun, such as behind bushes or trees in contact with the house. It may also be growing because of leaky gutters or downspouts, or perhaps from ice damming up in gutters so that water, which cannot be routed away properly, periodically flows down the siding.

Mildew can masquerade as ordinary dirt. To test it, dab household bleach on the suspicious spots. If the bleach makes the darkness disappear, it's mildew; if it doesn't, it's dirt. The only thing that kills mildew is bleach. You can do the removal and clean the house with detergent at the same time, using a bleach-water-detergent solution—one part detergent (without ammonia), ten parts household bleach, and thirty parts warm water. Before using this mix, protect any adjacent greenery with plastic drop cloths. Bleach kills plants.

You can apply the solution with a garden sprayer, mounting a ladder if necessary. You should wear waterproof protective gloves and protective eyewear, particularly if you are applying the bleach solution up high, such as on house siding where it can drop down onto your face. Do not allow the bleach solution to stay on the house more than ten minutes; do one side of the house at a time.

If you wish, you can get products that clean away mildew and soil in one fell swoop. Usually, the mildew remover comes as a concentrate that you mix with water and apply with a bristle brush. Follow the directions on the label for using the product. Normally, it is not necessary to scrub terribly hard nor to make the cleaning an all-day project.

> **Tip: Using Bleach**
> Don't mix bleach with a detergent containing ammonia. Doing so creates a toxic gas that can kill you.

Tannins

Tannins are extractive chemicals in certain woods, most commonly found in cedar and redwood, that bleed to the surface when the wood becomes wet, a process known as solubilization. They show up as brownish, blackish streaks and should be removed because they can bleed through the finish you apply. To make sure you're dealing with tannins, try the bleach test described in the previous section. If the darkness does not disappear, you have tannins or dirt.

OPPOSITE **Two coats of solid stain, preceded by a primer, will provide excellent protection for wood furniture in all kinds of weather.**

Sometimes rain washes them off, but if you are about to stain the surface and you want to get rid of them right away, you can do so by brushing on a cleaner that contains oxalic acid. These cleaners, which you mix with water, are widely available and will eliminate the tannins as well as soil. Check the container label. You'll probably see a statement that the cleaner contains oxalic acid, which is the main ingredient used in removing tannins. (Oxalic acid is also available in crystal form at drugstores—you mix it with water—but it's easier to use if you buy it as an ingredient in other cleaners.)

Iron Stains

Iron stains occur when nails rust or as a reaction of iron with tannins in the wood. The staining is usually caused by using low-quality nails, or it can result from screens or other steel items, such as air conditioners, coming in contact with the stain. If the stains are blue-black rather than the distinctive reddish color of rust, the stains are the result of tannins or other extractives in the wood interacting with steel nails or traces of steel left when cleaning the wood with steel wool or a wire brush. Commercially available cleaners containing oxalic acid also remove these stains.

Blue Stains

This type of stain is caused by microscopic fungi that commonly affect the sapwood of all woody species. Although microscopic, the fungi produce a blue-black discoloration. Blue stain does not normally affect a wood structurally, but conditions that favor blue stain development are also ideal for serious wood decay. Blue stain may be in the siding or in other wood, and nothing detrimental will happen as long as the moisture content is kept below twenty percent. However, if the wood is exposed to

> What about New Wood?

Just because wood is new doesn't make it clean. Lying around in the lumberyard can subject it to a variety of contaminants, including algae, dirt, mildew, tannins, and more. Before finishing it, it's best to clean it just as you would existing wood, even when no surface problems are obvious.

moisture from rain, condensation, or leaky plumbing, the moisture content will increase and the blue stain fungi will develop further with decay possibly following.

To prevent blue stain, keep the wood as dry as possible. Provide an adequate roof overhang and properly maintained shingles, gutters, and downspouts. Window and door casings should slope away from the house, allowing water to drain away rapidly. In northern climates, a vapor barrier inside the exterior walls prevents condensation. Also, vent clothes dryers, showers, and cooking areas to the outside. Be careful to avoid excess moisture buildup when using humidifiers.

Additionally, coat wood to protect it. To remove blue stain, the application of a five percent solution of sodium hypochlorite (liquid household bleach) sometimes removes blue stains, but it is not a permanent cure. The moisture problem must be corrected to achieve a permanent solution.

Brown Stains

The knots in many softwoods, particularly pine, contain much resin, and it can sometimes cause paint to

BELOW **Power washing is excellent for preparing a large deck, such as this one, for staining, but you have to control the pressure to prevent the water from scoring the wood.**

peel or turn brown. In most cases this is not a problem, though, because the resin is locked into the wood by the high temperatures used in the kiln-drying of lumber. Assuming you are using solid stain, a good staining practice stops brown stains before they start: Use a primer followed by two topcoats.

Exuding of Pitch

Pine and Douglas fir can exude pitch or resin, whereas cedar species, except western red cedar, can exude oils. Usually, pitch and oils are not a problem because manufacturers produce lumber at certain kiln-drying temperatures that lock the resin or pitch in place. Occasionally, however, it can be a problem.

If the boards are new and the pitch is dry, you can use a scraper to scrape it off. Follow up the scraping by sanding the wood. If the pitch is soft, use rags saturated with denatured alcohol to wipe away as much as you can, then sand the surface. If the wood still exudes pitch after this treatment, treat it again.

If the wood is exuding pitch after you've stained it, it might be best to leave it alone until it is time to restain. At that time the pitch can be scraped off and the areas sanded and primed. If the stain has peeled badly, it might be best to replace the boards before restaining. Pitch can continue to exude from boards for years, with no way to stop it. The condition is usually exacerbated during months when the weather is hot.

Peeling Paint

You can get peeling paint off a surface in various ways. In most cases, a stiff-bladed 3" (7.6 cm) scraper does the job. If the surfaces are peeling fairly heavily, a hook-type scraper can be enlisted to remove it.

To use the tool, grasp it firmly and pull it down the wood, applying pressure as you go. This process should pull off the paint. Some models of this scraper also have a knob on top for gripping with one hand and providing even more pressure. As you go, examine the surface for areas where peeling may take place—the paint is bubbly or raised—and scrape them off. You can test suspicious areas with tape. Cut through the paint film with a utility knife, place tape or an adhesive bandage over it. Pull the tape away quickly to see if the paint adheres. If it does, the paint should be removed.

When you scrape in this way, you are often left with a shallow, cratered surface. Use exterior spackling compound to fill in the craters, or at least apply it along the edges and feather the compound out so the edges are not noticeable. Finish by sanding smooth.

Machine-Sanding

For large peeling areas, the best and fastest way to remove the peeling stain is with a sander. Using two kinds of paper, 16-grit and 60-grit, is a good choice. The 16-grit sandpaper removes all the peeling paint down to the bare wood. The 60-grit paper smoothes any grooves or rough spots left in the wood by the 16-grit paper. It is important not to leave any paint on the surface after rough sanding; it will clog the pores of the 60-grit material.

The idea in sanding is to leave a surface on which the new solid-color stain will adhere as well as one that looks good before beginning. Use a nail set and hammer to set any loose nails or ones whose heads are not flush in the wood. Sanding over a protruding nail head can tear the sandpaper and damage the hard rubber drum to which the sandpaper is attached.

Use a rotary sander, but be careful to follow the grain—it can heavily score the surface. Turn on the machine, and bring it to the work surface while it is moving. Move it along the surface, holding it a few degrees (up to 10°) off the surface. Do not press it flush to the surface, because it tends to pull out of your hands and can be hard to manage.

ABOVE **A stiff-blade scraper can remove lightly peeling paint. Just push the blade up into the peeling surface.**

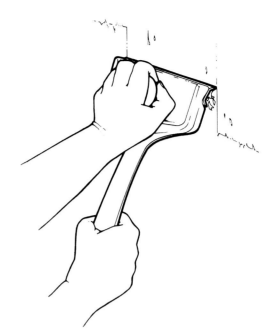

ABOVE **A hook-type scraper works best for extensively peeling paint. It also allows you to apply more force.**

Preparing Painted Surfaces

Chalking

Some paint is manufactured so it "chalks"—a microscopic amount of it in the form of powder is washed off by precipitation. This characteristic keeps the surface fresh looking. However, sometimes chalking is excessive, and the chalk flows down and streaks surfaces below it. These streaks are commonly seen on masonry from the chalk having been washed off the siding above.

A certain amount of chalking is desirable because it keeps the surface looking new. However, excessive chalking is not desirable. Also, if you use solid-color stain on the painted surface without proper preparation, the stain can fail because it is not adhering well enough to the surface.

If you have chalk streaks, the area above should be scrubbed with a detergent solution to remove the deposits. (You will be removing soil as well.) After scrubbing or power washing the siding, rinse it thoroughly with clear water. (Alternatively, you can rent a scrub brush with a whirling bristle section to get very high areas, or climb up on a ladder.) Let it dry, then test to see how much chalk is left. If the chalking surface is white, rub a dark cloth on it. If dark, rub a white cloth. In either case, if you see chalk, then that is the amount you can expect in terms of future chalking. At any rate, you should always apply a primer before applying two coats of solid-color stain. To remove any chalk streaks that have gotten on masonry, use a detergent-water solution.

> **Tip:** No matter what kind of cleaning you perform on wood, you should always rinse the surface when you're finished and let it dry completely before applying any finish.

LEFT **Decking is made from a variety of wood species. Your local lumber dealer can make suggestions as to what types are available in your area. Consider the look you like best and what type of stain you plan to use before making your selection.**

Other Blemishes

The surface to be stained must be clean. A rogue's gallery of blemishes and some homemade methods of removing them follows below. You can also find commercially available wood cleaners that will clean these things. Check the label of the product you buy to confirm this.

Algae and Moss

Algae and moss leave green stains that are difficult to remove completely. They develop a root structure, which penetrates the wood and can regrow. One way to control them is to apply bleach full strength as needed, but be sure to rinse with clear water after you're finished. Pure bleach can damage wood.

Wax

When citronella and other candles are used in and around a deck, you may have wax drippings. Place a rag saturated with mineral-spirits (paint thinner) on the wax spot, and keep it wet until the wax is absorbed into the rag.

Barbecue Sauce, Grease, and Fats

Clean these with any water-rinsable automotive degreaser or carburetor cleaner. Do not apply these removers when the surface is exposed to direct sun—use only in the shade.

Leaf Stains

Wash with a one-to-one solution of household bleach and water. Rinse thoroughly.

OPPOSITE **Priming is one of the key elements in a successful solid-stain job, especially when a dramatic color change is desired, such as going from a darker color to white.**

> Choice of Woods

In some cases, deck boards or other parts must be replaced. If you have a choice of woods for repair, consider using a decay-resistant species. Ideally, this wood would be what is known as old-growth type, which means that it has been growing for decades, even hundreds of years. So-called second-growth timber—trees more recently planted—is not as decay resistant, but there's no way to distinguish the two at the lumberyard. Decay-resistant woods include:

- Bald cypress (old growth)
- Catalpa
- Cedar
- Cherry (black)
- Chestnut
- Cypress (Arizona)
- Juniper
- Locust (black)
- Mesquite
- Mulberry (red)
- Oak (bur, chestnut, Gambel, Oregon white, post, white)
- Osage (orange)
- Redwood
- Sassafras
- Walnut (black)
- Yew (Pacific)

Lumber-grading Stamps

There is no way to effectively remove these, although you can cover them with a primer when you use solid-color stain. If you intend to coat the wood with a semitransparent material, sand off the numbers and letters.

Preparation Steps

Power Washing

Many houses, decks, fences, and other surfaces turn gray because of mildew or the effects of sunlight. If you want to clean off the gray and return the house to its original natural color, a good way to do it is with a power washer—a gas- or electrical-powered machine. (See chapter two, page 38, for more on power washers.) The power washer drives water against a surface at high pressure and in great volume and is capable of everything from removing the gray to blasting paint off a surface. Because it is a powerful machine, however, you must take care with it. If you use too high a pressure you can score the wood and the stain won't take evenly.

If you are just cleaning a painted surface or if you're going to apply a solid-color stain and want to remove tannins or mildew, buy a solution for use in the power washer that includes bleach in its formula and, thus, kills mildew. Make sure to buy a ready-made product. Manufacturers who put bleach in their products also add anticorrosive agents. Without these, the bleach could destroy the internal rubber parts of the machine.

ABOVE **Check your decking surfaces regularly for boards that are beginning to loosen because of aging nails. Replacing with stainless or galvanized screws solves the problem and prevents future rust damage.**

If you are power washing asbestos cement shingles, vinyl siding, metal siding, or other nonwood products, just spray away with pressure at about 1,000 psi and using two to three gallons (7.6 to 11.4 liters) per minute of water. However, if you are power washing a softwood, such as cedar or redwood, be extremely careful not to score the wood. Use low pressure and work up to a pressure that you can see does not score the wood. Some people use 1,000 psi; others use 2,000 psi and even more. The key is to keep the spray wand moving.

Power washing transfers a tremendous amount of water to the surface, so make sure the wood has a couple of days to dry thoroughly before you apply the stain. You can hold the power washer wand as close as needed to get the job done, but if the siding is clapboard or wood shingles, angle the spray so that water does not drive up under the courses or shingles, which can set up a moisture-laden environment ripe for mildew formation. Spray from a ladder to guard against this.

Both hot and cold water models are available. The hot-water model does a better job of removing baked-in dirt. Various wands are available, and these are invaluable for focusing the stream. Regarding pressure, you need the capability to go to 3,000 or 4,000 pounds per square inch if you expect to clean concrete; just be very careful if using them on wood.

Caulking

If you are staining a house you should first use caulk to fill the seams of the house, such as joints where windows and trim meet siding. A number of caulks are available, but not all of them are mildew resistant—something you should check for on the label. Silicone is the best caulk you can buy. No matter what type you use, do understand that clear coatings and semi-transparent stain will not penetrate it. Happily, caulk is available in a variety of colors. Just pick the color closest to your stain color. Caulk made of latex with acrylic is cheaper and is also available in a variety of colors. It accepts solid-color stain.

Before you caulk, scrape out all old material with an opener. The new material is only as good as the material under it. Use an old paint brush or a dust brush made for the job to get out any material that has crumbled. Crumbled caulk does not make for a solid surface.

To apply caulking from a gun, cut the cartridge tip at a slant so that a slanted opening in the nozzle of the cartridge allows a wide bead of caulk to be extruded. Puncture the inner seal on the cartridge with a long nail or a slim piece of wood.

Insert the cartridge in the caulking gun, and then put the tip of the nozzle on top of the area to be caulked. Squeeze the trigger with even pressure, and as you do, draw the gun down along the crack in one continuous motion, extruding a bead that is one-half as deep as it is wide. The bead should be concave. To ensure this, draw a spoon along it, or simply use your forefinger.

In some cases, the gaps are so deep that a bead of caulk alone will not be enough—a filler material of some sort has to be inserted. One type of filler (such as Mortite), comes in long, beaded strips that can be ripped off as needed. Just press the material in place with your fingers—it will stick—and then apply the caulk. You can also use fiberglass insulation or a foam-backed rod. If the gaps are very big, there are foams that come in a can (such as Great Stuff) and can be used to partially fill the crack. Squirt some into the gap, and as it dries, it expands. Foam should be applied sparingly until you get a sense of how much is required, because a little, when dry, can go a long way.

Priming Painted Wood

If you are using solid-color stain, you can use the same techniques for priming the wood as you would for applying paint. A number of primers are available for the job, both latex and oil-based. Pros favor oil-based. Follow the recommendations of your dealer.

If you are making a dramatic color change—say, going from yellow to green—a primer is a good idea. A latex primer works quite well, assuming the wood is a nonbleeding type, such as pine. To ensure that the topcoat covers better, tint the primer with universal

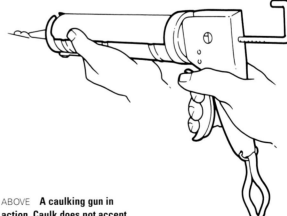

ABOVE **A caulking gun in action. Caulk does not accept stain, so your best bet is to find a caulk that is as close as possible to the color of your stain.**

colorant. Normally, up to four ounces (120 ml) per gallon of color can be added without causing the color to streak. A primer, of course, provides an excellent basecoat for the topcoat.

If portions of the paint film have been removed, exposing bare wood, spot-prime these first, allow them to dry, then prime the entire house.

If you are painting nonbleeding new woods (not cedar or redwood), then you can use latex primer. If you are painting patched areas on bleeding woods, such as cedar or redwood, standard latex primer is not recommended. The water in the primer can solubilize tannins in the wood and send them to the surface, where they will discolor the primer and may not be covered by the topcoat.

An oil-based primer is recommended for bleeding woods like cedar and redwood because the oils in it will not solubilize the extracts in the wood. (One water-based primer, Bulls Eye 1-2-3, is recommended for use on bleeding woods.)

Repairs

Inevitably, wood structures, such as decks and fencing, need repair. A lineup of some commonly needed repairs follows:

Loose Deck Boards

This situation occurs when boards have pulled loose from their framing. Usually, the culprit is loose nails. As people walk on the boards they gradually work free.

You could hammer the nails back into position, but there's no guarantee that they will hold. A much better solution is to use corrosion-resistant screws— stainless steel or high-quality galvanized—to pull the loose board or boards tightly together. Drive the screws in with an electric drill so they are $\frac{1}{4}$" (0.6 cm) or so beneath the surface, then use wood filler to fill the depressions.

Sometimes, a board may be split. Here, use a screwdriver or other scraper to open the crack a little further, then squirt in water-resistant glue and pull the

ABOVE **When boards loosen, the best solution is to reset them with corrosion-resistant screws. If you wish, you can also get screws in various colors to match wood components.**

ABOVE **Sometimes a split board can be repaired by first injecting weatherproof glue in the crack, then clamping it together until dry, perhaps by wrapping duct tape around it.**

pieces together with either clamps or by wrapping duct tape tightly around them. Or, you can loop cord around the loose pieces, then tie the ends of the cord to a small piece of wood and twist it around so the cord gradually wraps tighter and tighter around the cracked board. Allow the glue to dry for twenty-four hours.

Sagging Fence Gate

If a gate on a fence is sagging, the best way to straighten it out is with a turnbuckle support, which attaches to framing members and then is tightened in the middle with a wrench, gradually pulling framing members into proper position and aligning the gate.

Holes

Wood siding and trim, as well as deck railing and fencing, can be susceptible to a variety of holes. If you are using solid-color stain, then you can fill the holes, dab on a prime coat of the stain, allow it to dry, and then apply the finish coat. Small holes can be filled with exterior spackling compound and then touched up with a coat of the finish stain.

If the hole or gap is large and there is rot present, say, on a window frame, then spackling compound is not enough. A product that fills the hole and prevents further problems is needed. One such product is Minwax Wood Filler. First, scrape out the rot with a stiff putty knife, then mix the filler—a two-part material—and apply it to the damaged area, just as you would any filler. After drying—it dries very hard—sand, prime, and paint it.

Another standard wood filler for exterior (and interior) work is Durham's Rock Hard Water Putty, which comes as a yellowish powder that is mixed with water into a thick paste. Apply the paste and let it dry into a rock-hard material that can be sanded, primed, and painted or coated with solid-color stain. Mix it in the same way as you would mix plaster. Pour it into a container, such as a tin plate. Use a trowel to depress it in the center, and pour water into the crater. Then use the scraper to fold the water and putty together, mixing it completely. Add water sparingly until it is the right consistency. If you add too much water, just add more powder to thicken it up.

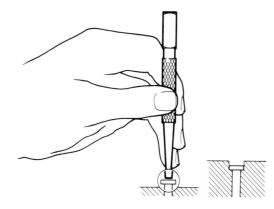

ABOVE **Preparing the surface includes driving exposed nails beneath the surface with a nail set. Set it on the nail head and hammer it to countersink it.**

ABOVE **If a hole or split in wood is small, use a stainable wood filler. When the stain is applied, the wood accepts it like surrounding wood and the repair is not obvious.**

Avoid air pockets in the patcher. Push in the patcher with the scraper, or use your fingers to work it in. Another patching material that is quite good, perhaps the best material for the job, is made by Arbatron.

Any protruding nails can be countersunk with a nail set and hammer and the depressions filled with compound. If the hole is small and a clear coating is going to be applied over it, then a wood filler is recommended. Although there is no such thing as a perfect match, fillers are available in a wide variety of wood colors and are easy to apply with a putty knife. If you are using a penetrating stain, get the stainable kind. Here, the stain penetrates the patcher just as it does the surrounding wood. If the hole is very extensive, you can either hire a carpenter or install new shingles or whatever wood needs replacement yourself. Home improvement warehouses carry all manner of materials that can be used for replacement. In some cases, replacement of a shingle or board is required.

Structural Problems

As time goes by, particular problems can develop with decks, but they all boil down to one thing: parts become loose. If this is the case, screws are the way to go. Before driving the screw, kneel on the loose board so it is in close contact with the structural members below, and then drive the screw in. Loose steps can be handled the same way. If there is any sway to a deck, use framing fasteners to provide more stability.

Covering Up

Preparation for staining includes covering up. If you are spraying, it's a good idea to completely cover windows with plastic sheeting held on with painter's tape. You can buy machines to apply the tape. Bushes should be covered, as should screens and anything else that stain could fall on.

As mentioned earlier, if you are spraying on the stain, by all means make sure the overspray does not float onto nearby cars or other items.

OPPOSITE **Before starting a staining job, cover nearby surfaces, such as windows, stonework, and shrubbery, so stain won't get on them and cause damage.**

> **Good Points to Remember**

• Before applying a penetrating stain to wood, sprinkle some water on the wood to see if it is absorbed. If the water is not absorbed, the wood needs further preparation.

• To see if there is debris—such as loose paint or loose fibers—on a surface, do the adhesive bandage test—adhere the bandage, then tear it off and see if it has anything stuck to it.

• Remove mill glaze with light sanding.

• Tannins are unsightly. They look tea colored but turn black and can bleed through a new finish. Once you've determined you have tannins, remove them with a solution containing oxalic acid.

• You can buy stainable wood filler or find it in colors to blend with the material you're using.

• If you have rot, get a product designed to stop it, such as Minwax High Performance filler or Arbatron. You can also use a wood hardener, which is pumped into rotting wood to stop further deterioration.

• Use a nail set to drive all nail heads beneath the surface, then fill the holes with stainable filler.

• Cover up completely before you start the job. You don't want to have to stop to reset drop cloths.

CHAPTER 4

Stripping Wood

In some cases, a surface coating may be in such bad shape that it has to be completely removed before you can apply a stain. The coating may be peeling to such an extent that scraping and sanding or even using a machine sander is not enough to complete the job.

You may want to strip a surface because you do not like the existing color. Of course you can change the color by covering it with a solid stain or paint, but you may want a clear coating or a semitransparent stain on the wood rather than a solid color. The only solution is taking the existing coating off down to bare wood. The removers available these days will do an outstanding job. Don't be discouraged if you are inheriting a terrible paint job—a removal may expose a beautiful natural wood underneath.

Any kind of finish can be removed from any kind of surface. Probably the most common surface is decking, but people also redo furniture, sheds, accessories, doors, and even siding. Companies who make stains usually also make stain removers, and current products are quite effective. As with everything, you should read the labels carefully to ensure that the product is designed to do what you need it to.

OPPOSITE **By following all the necessary steps in the stripping procedure, you will break down the old material and prepare the surface for a first-rate stain application.**

Removing stain or paint was once a difficult, nasty job. You worked with toxic chemicals that were dangerous to breathe, no less to touch. But those days are gone forever. Now many manufacturers have formulated a new breed of safe, effective formulations. These products are specifically designed to remove a wide variety of exterior finishes, including solid-color and semitransparent stains, varnishes, water repellents, urethanes, and wood preservatives. What's more, most of these deck strippers are biodegradable and safe to use near plants and shrubs. Once the old finish is removed, you can use a brightener to return the wood to its original color. Indeed, the results are quite dramatic—and quite satisfying.

BELOW **Today's strippers can do a terrific job stripping off all kinds of finishes. Here, a portion of a deck is covered with solid stain.**

ABOVE **The same section of deck after the stain was stripped off. The wood looks brand-new and ready to accept all kinds of stain.**

Challenge

In the photo sequence shown here, one of these products, Bio-Wash, was used to remove three coats of gray semitransparent oil-based stain from a red cedar deck. Other brands are also good. Just read the label to make sure that the stripper is strong enough to do the job and is biodegradable.

Here, a product named Stripex-L, a Bio-Wash product, was used. The thick, water-based gel is easy to control yet powerful enough to work quickly. One gallon strips about 150 square feet (13.9 square meters) of decking. The plastic jug comes with a packet of deck brightener, too.

The first step was testing to make sure the stripper would work on the finish. A little of the material was applied to an area 6" (15.2 cm) square and then misted with water to initiate the chemical action. After about fifteen minutes, an old chisel was used to scrape the stripper and coatings beneath to see if the stripper was working and to determine the waiting time required before attempting to wash it off. The test was successful. The stripper had already softened all three coats of stain.

Applying the Stripper

The first step in stripping the entire deck was to use a garden hose to wet all the surrounding vegetation, including the grass. Although strippers can be non-toxic and biodegradable, it's still wise to protect the plants in case they get splashed with a full-strength dose of the product. Next, pour the stripper into a plastic bucket and apply it to the decking with a paint roller fitted onto an extension handle. Then, mist the decking with water from a garden hose to activate the stripper. Misting the surface is a critical step, because the stripper is effective only when it's wet.

After about ten minutes, scrub the surface of the wood with a long-handled brush to break down the stain and speed up the process. After fifteen minutes, scrape a small section of deck with a chisel to see if the stripper has worked its way down to bare wood.

Removing the Stripper

To remove the stripper and old stain, use a power washer and a spray wand fitted with a 25-degree fan tip; set the water pressure to 2,000 psi. To avoid damaging the wood when using this much pressure, constantly move the wand and hold it far enough from the wood so it doesn't score it. Just as important, don't point it at anyone—it can produce a deep wound.

If you don't own a power washer, you can rent one. You could also rinse off the stripper with a gar-den hose, though a hose, which generates far less water pressure, takes considerably longer than a power washer.

After washing off the old finish, use a paintbrush to apply stripper between deck boards, beneath the front edge of steps, and other spots the roller can't reach. Sprinkle any residual stain with water and, after 15 minutes, blast it off with the power washer.

Mix a 6-ounce (170.1-gram) packet of powdered brightener into $\frac{1}{2}$ gallon (1.9 liters) of water, and then brush the solution onto the stripped deck boards. You can use the brush to scrub the brightener into the

BELOW **Before starting a stripping job, wet down surrounding vegetation. Even though the material you use is biodegradable, consider it extra insurance.**

BELOW **Here, stripper is applied with a paint roller over the entire deck, then allowed to set up according to the time specified on the container.**

BELOW **Next, the entire deck was misted with water. For this product, misting is crucial because it works only when wet.**

BELOW **After the desk was misted, it was scrubbed with a stiff-bristled broom to agitate and loosen the stain.**

surface and, after about ten minutes, rinse it off with the power washer. Once the deck has dried, protect it with two coats of a clear wood preservative. You can also restain it.

Strippers work amazingly well. One slow pass with the power washer over each board exposes bare, clean wood. Because strippers darken the wood, you'll need to use the deck brightener included with it. Besides lightening the surface of the wood, the brightener neutralizes any stripper left on the surface.

BELOW **After allowing the stripper to work for the specified time, scrape a small area to see if it has loosened the stain below. If it has, you're ready to begin the removal.**

BELOW **Use a small brush to apply stripper where the roller can't reach, such as between deck boards and the front of steps.**

BELOW **Use a power washer to blast off the loosened stain. Take great care not to score wood. Use a proper wand and keep the jet spray moving.**

> What about Heat?

Heat is another way to remove paint or stain. But as a popular do-it-yourself manual points out, any tool that comes with ten pages of instructions is something to be wary of. There are a couple of reasons for this.

For one thing, heat could cause a fire. Many heat guns, also called hot air guns and electric paint strippers, operate at temperatures in excess of 1,200°F (648.9°C). That is hot enough to set paper, wood, and cloth on fire, and certainly hot enough to burn you badly. Personally, I don't recommend them, particularly when environmentally safe chemicals are available. Of course, pros use them, but they have lots of experience.

> Good Points to Remember

- The new generation of strippers are safe to use yet very powerful.

- Even though the stripper you use may be biodegradable, soak the surrounding vegetation to protect it should some stripper splash onto it, particularly because you'll be using a power washer.

- Wear goggles and gloves. Even the safest strippers can irritate eyes and skin.

- Try to work in the shade. Keeping the stripper active means keeping it wet. Sunlight evaporates and weakens it.

- Apply the stripper at the rate the manufacturer recommends.

- Don't reroll areas where the stripper has been applied.

- Brush on the stripper slowly and carefully. Don't crisscross strokes or go over previously rolled areas.

- Don't walk on areas that are coated with stripper—they're very slippery.

- Strip large or multilevel decks in small sections to keep the process manageable.

- Keep strippers away from bare-metal surfaces, such as aluminum thresholds or screen doors, because it tarnishes them.

BELOW **The final step is to apply a wood brightener, which comes in a powder and is mixed with water. Stripping tends to darken wood.**

CHAPTER 5

Staining Decks

Of all the surfaces in or around the house, the deck takes more abuse than any other. Part of this battering comes from the sun, which contains UV rays that degrade the fibers of the wood, specifically the lignin that holds those fibers together. Because of its position in relation to the sun, the deck takes the most direct punishment from its rays. Siding, on the other hand, is on an angle to the sun, so it gets much less of the sun's direct rays.

Water also gives a deck a pummeling. Not only does rain (and in some climates, snow) fall directly on a deck, it stays there. Water "ponds" to some degree on the boards and snow melts. At certain times, especially in wet climates, it's almost as if the deck is under water for days. Decks that are built low to the ground are in close proximity to insects. Low-lying decks also trap the moisture from evaporating water, which creates an environment perfect for the development of fungi.

Then, of course, there is traffic. In the good-weather months, the deck is often used more than the rooms inside the house. In addition, it bears traffic from people with sand on their feet or stones in their shoes and from the moving around of patio furniture, potted plants, toys, and the barbecue grill. All this abrasive activity does a lot to wear out the applied product.

OPPOSITE **The natural effect of semitransparent stain is enhanced by the landscape and wood accents of this country home.**

BELOW **A deck coated with semitransparent stain. The key ingredient in the stain is the resins, which are "harder curing," as chemists say, than the resins used for siding.**

But these types of assault are not the only problem. Most existing decks (there are, incidentally, thirty million of them in existence, with more being built every day) were built with the now-outlawed pressure-treated wood. Whereas pressure-treated wood is fine to protect against mildew and insects, the lower-grade woods used to make it, such as southern yellow pine, were used because the chromated copper arsenate preservative does not penetrate higher-quality woods such as cedar and redwood. Hence, you start out with an inferior product that regularly splits, and once a horizontal deck board has split, it is virtually impossible to keep it whole for any length of time. Water gets into the cracks and saturates the wood, resulting in swelling.

Old Growth versus Second-Growth Wood

Another issue for deck refinishing is that the best quality woods come from old-growth forests, meaning 200 years old or more, and the harvesting of this wood has been virtually eliminated in this country, leaving only second-growth forests as a lumber source. Second-growth forests contain, in addition to younger trees, smaller, faster-growing hybrid trees that, collectively, have more undesirable sapwood and knots and less of the desirable heartwood—wood from the center of the tree. Milling procedures for these smaller trees produce boards that are the most difficult to coat successfully.

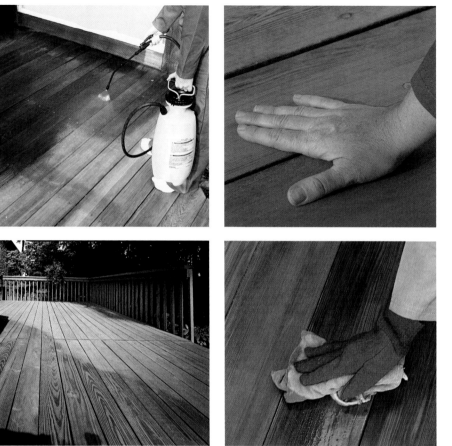

FAR LEFT **A garden sprayer is a good tool with which to apply stain, but you must backbrush it into the wood as you go to ensure penetration.**

LEFT **You should not apply deck stain in the sun if you can help it and certainly not when the deck is hot to the touch. Check it out before beginning.**

FAR LEFT **A deck half-coated with semitransparent stain. As you can see, it makes a huge difference in the way the wood looks. If a clear coating was used, the deck would only look as if it were wet.**

LEFT **Here, a rag is used to wipe up an oil-based semi-transparent stain. The rag is handy for wiping up excess stain, which you don't want to leave on a deck because it can form a film.**

In addition, mahogany and similar woods such as Port Oxford white cedar, peroba de campos, and ipe are now frequently used to build decks. These woods are problematic because they don't absorb a protective stain well, if at all. For example, mahogany (which is available in many different species) is rich in natural oils that make it very resistant to decay. However, because of this and the high density of the heartwood, it also makes it very difficult for stains to penetrate or for solid stains to adhere. Also, mahogany is quite dimensionally unstable, which causes the top fibers to become loose in exterior applications. The weather can also cause warping, splitting, cracking, and delaminating of the grain. No coating could hold such a wood together. Ipe—the heartwood of the Tabebuia species—is so dense and heavy that it often sinks in water. It is virtually impenetrable by liquids, including water.

A Dangerous Myth

As detailed in chapter three, one reason for coating failure is lack of proper preparation. But there is another common reason for failure, namely, the myth that a newly built deck should be allowed to weather for a long period of time before being coated.

The reasoning behind this myth is that by letting the wood weather or dry out, it will somehow become more receptive to absorbing stain. So some people let the wood weather six months or even a year before coating it. I don't recommended this. Uncoated wood starts to become damaged by weather, chiefly water, very quickly—even within weeks.

So, how long should you wait? Read the label of the stain you choose. The time varies from product to product, but manufacturers generally recommend coating within a few days and usually within thirty days at the very outside.

ABOVE **Here a brush is used to apply stain. The key is to work small areas at a time, keeping a wet edge to avoid lapmarks.**

ABOVE **If you don't want to bend over while applying stain, use a pad on a stick or a staining brush, into which the stick can be screwed.**

> ### > Tip: Using the Same Color

One advantage of using solid-color stain is that you can use the same exact color on the siding that you can on the deck. There aren't any paints available to do the same thing.

Applying Stain

Whatever the material you are applying to the deck, you should first get it machine-agitated wherever you buy it. This is particularly important if you purchased semitransparent material or toner, because you want to make sure that the pigment is distributed evenly throughout. And if you do the job with a penetrating stain, stir it frequently.

How you specifically do the job will depend on the material you are using, but it also depends on what the manufacturer recommends. Most importantly: read the label. For example, after spraying, one manufacturer may recommend following that with backbrushing, while a different company may recommend letting the stain penetrate the surface for fifteen minutes to a half hour, and then wiping off the excess with a rag.

In addition to following the manufacturer's advice, here are some general tips:

- Avoid over-application—This is a frequent mistake people make with clear coatings, toners, and semi-transparent stains. The logic is, if some stain is good, a lot of stain has to be great. Wrong. The wood can absorb only a certain amount of the product at one time, and if you put on too much you can end up with a lot of the stain not absorbing, resulting in a sticky mess on the surface.

- Work in the shade as much as possible—It's easier on you and keeps the stain wetter, preventing the formation of lap marks.

OPPOSITE **To avoid lapmarks, work in the shade whenever possible when applying stain. Heat from sunlight promotes quicker drying time and reduces your ability to maintain a "wet edge."**

> Good Points to Remember

- Before purchasing a product for your deck, check the can's label to make sure it is formulated for use on a deck.

- A deck takes more abuse than any other part of a house, chiefly from water. Coating it can add years to its life.

- Before leaving a store with the stain, have the dealer machine-agitate it to make sure that the contents are well mixed.

- A garden sprayer makes a quick applicator for penetrating stain, but the stain must then be backbrushed.

- If you see excess stain ponding on the surface, use a rag to wipe it up.

- Don't overapply stain. Follow the manufacturer's directions.

- Frequently stir penetrating stain as you go to make sure solids and solvents are well mixed.

- If you can, try to work in the shade. It is easier on you and also helps you avoid overlaps.

- If you want to use a pad or staining brush, attach it to a stick so you don't have to bend over.

- Work small areas when applying stain. It's easier to control.

- Plan your escape route—Plan the job and how you will work your way around. You don't want to stain yourself into a corner.

- Start with the railings—Put a couple of drop cloths around the posts so you don't drip stain on the deck boards. (You don't want unsightly drops showing.) Also put drop cloths over vegetation so it doesn't look speckled when you're finished. If you need to do any masking, adhere some blue painter's tape to the area you want to protect (such as the bottom of siding boards adjacent to the deck).

  Once the railings are done, apply the stain to the lengths of boards. Start at one end, and begin applying it with a brush, roller, or painting pad, following directions on the can. Work small areas, two to three boards at a time, covering about 3" or 4" (0.9 m or 1.2 m). No matter what kind of stain you use, coat an area only where you can constantly keep what painters call a wet edge. Work your way across the length of the deck, then back the other way. What you want to avoid is a situation where you come back with a fresh brushful of stain and apply it to the edge of the previously applied material and the edge has already flash-dried. This can happen very quickly in the sun, particularly if the product has a lot of solvent in it, such as clear coatings, toners, and semitransparent stains do. In effect, it's like applying two coats there, and the lap mark will show.

- The best tool with which to apply toners, semitransparent, and clear coatings is a usually brush. It allows you to work the product into the wood pores. Pads on a stick work well also.

- Maintain proper staining order: On a staircase, do the railings first, then the steps.

CHAPTER 6

Staining Houses and Sheds

You'll really appreciate it when you start using stain instead of paint. The material is simply a lot easier to use, and when you're up against finishing a large area, you'll appreciate it that much more.

This chapter covers not only how to stain a home, but also smaller structures such as sheds. It's important not to regard various outbuildings as completely independent structures when considering color, but as a part of the entire property.

The section also covers how to stain log houses, which have become increasingly popular in recent years and benefit from having a protective coating applied to them. Some logs houses last more than a hundred years. That's a long time. Many would last even longer if they were maintained with a proper finish.

Some people prefer to use paint for the trim of homes and outbuildings and stain on the siding. There are instructions for using this option if you wish. You will also find information on how to stain difficult parts of a house, such as dormers, which are often trickier to coat than straight siding.

There are also details on the more sophisticated kinds of equipment that are available for staining a large project such as a house. Many pros favor spraying equipment—you spray the material on first, and then backbrush—and if you learn to use the equipment well enough (you might start with the shed), you'll find that the job goes very quickly indeed.

OPPOSITE **This outbuilding has added character thanks to the contrasting stain colors. The choice of hues makes the garden setting even more inviting.**

Staining the exterior of a building or home is usually more difficult than the interior, particularly if you have to use an extension ladder. The up-and-down aspect is physically taxing, as is moving the ladder. You also must be careful not to spill stain and be mindful of safety, avoiding falls and electrical hazards.

You can do a number of things to make a job easier. As always, stay in the shade as much as possible. It is better for the stain and for the stainer, because, as mentioned previously, direct sunlight on freshly applied stain can drying the material quickly and lead to lap marks, which can be a problem anyway with penetrating stains, simply because they dry quickly, sun or no sun. Staining in the shade is not always possible; if you must stain in the sun, try to do it early in the morning, when you and the surface are not receiving the direct rays of the sun.

Also, to guard against lap marks when using a penetrating stain, select areas to stain that are small enough that you can coat them completely before the edges start drying. For example, do a section of boards from the end of the house to a window frame. This way you can likely keep the entire area wet until finished.

When staining a house, it's best to start in an area that is least visible. This way, if you make a mistake, it won't be out front for everyone to see. In addition, work from the top down. If stain drips as you go, brush it out quickly and completely, then immediately finish the section or board the drip was on so you won't have to stain over it and risk a lap mark.

Most people do the siding first and then the trim. The reason is that a lot of stain is applied when siding is done, and some drips and spatters are bound to land on the trim. If so, the drips can be wiped up and then coated when the trim is finished. Doing it in this order means having to lean a ladder against freshly stained siding. This is not usually a problem if the ends of the ladder are covered with ladder mitts or wrap with rags.

Covering Up

Canvas drop cloths work best for covering up. They drape over things more easily and do not flutter away in the wind. Second best are heavy plastic drop cloths. Cover anything anywhere you figure the stain may fall and anywhere you are likely to walk. Be particularly careful to cover asphalt roofing. Because these items are porous, removing errant drops of stain can be a problem. Getting stain off screens is difficult as well. Therefore, it is always a good idea to remove the screens or to drape cloths or drape or tape newspapers over them.

Try not to cover plants, flowers, and bushes for too long. Being covered by drop cloths is not a natural situation for vegetation, and the sooner you allow air and sunlight in, the better. If bushes and plants are brushing against a wall, cover them with drop cloths and tie them back a bit with rope or just hold them back with your back as you slither through.

> **Tip:** To conserve energy, take breaks, drink plenty of cool liquids, and don't overexert yourself. Again, try not to work in the sun.

Masking Off Windows and Doors

Some do-it-yourselfers mask off windows and doors when they stain; others do not, thinking it will take them a lot longer. Masking off is a good idea, but do not use masking tape on a painted surface because it can strip off paint. Use painter's tape, which looks and works the same as masking tape but strips off easily without pulling off the finish. You can use it along a roofline where you will be cutting in, such as where a dormer cuts into a roof, and around posts mounted in concrete. In other words, put tape wherever you need a sharp, clean line and where the stained surface meets the unstained, such as where a dormer meets roof shingles. When staining these cut-in areas, I have always found it best to use a "dry" brush—one that has stain on it but does not drip. Even though the painter's tape protects the surface, you do not want stain to run down onto it. Wait until the stain is dry before you strip off the tape so the stain does not come off with the tape.

You can also protect roof shingles by forcing a plastic or cloth drop a little way under the adjacent siding, pushing the drop cloth in with a scraper. Apply the stain to the siding and, after it has dried, pull the drop cloth out.

Applying the Stain

If you are using a clear coating, semitransparent, or other penetrating stain, you should apply the material with a brush, staining pad, or, as detailed later, a sprayer, then backbrush when you're finished. If you are using solid-color stain you can, as indicated earlier, handle and apply it as if it were house paint. The easiest way to paint siding is to do as much of it with a sprayer or, if the manufacturer allows, a roller and use a brush to cut in around windows, doors, and other things protruding from the siding (such as vents and pipes). Remember to keep a wet edge.

Siding Overview

The following list covers various siding types and some methods that can be employed to stain them with solid-color stain:

Asbestos Cement Shingles

Staining asbestos cement shingles is a good job for a roller. A $\frac{3}{4}$"- (1.9-cm) nap works well, but I know one painter who swears by $1\frac{1}{2}$"- (3.8-cm) nap, saying that because it brings so much stain to the surface, the job goes more quickly. This thick of a nap can leave a textured finish, but backrolling would solve this.

Concentrate on getting a generous amount of stain on the surface, applying it in W or M patterns, in a 3' (91.4-cm) strip that goes from the bottom to the top of the siding. Do an adjacent 3' (91.4-cm) strip in the same way, and then come back with a dry roller and backroll the applied stain in the first strip until it is smooth.

Cedar Siding

If you have the flat type of cedar siding, you can apply solid-color stain using a small 3" to 4"- (7.6-cm to 10.2-cm) wide roller, rolling on the stain horizontally. If the siding is striated, use a brush or a pad to apply the material vertically.

Staining striated cedar siding is basically a wipe-down job. Dip the applicator into the stain, jam it up under the shingles, and wipe the stain on with a downward stroke. Old-time painters often use a "stub" brush for this, which is a cut-down or worn, old brush, but a paint pad works well, too. Look for a pad with thick, fluffy naps as well as one with a rough texture and a turned-over fabric. The turned-over portion is designed to be jammed under a course of shingles.

Clapboard

Clapboard is made up of boards 3" to 4" (7.6 cm to 10.2 cm) high or higher. First, cut in the overlapping boards, then apply the stain with a small roller or pad. If the clapboard is deeper, you can use a roller or a pad.

Staining Difficult Areas

Not all houses are single-story ranches and simple to finish. Some have all kinds of angles that make staining some spots difficult.

Dormers

One difficult area is the sides of dormers or similar configurations. The roof slants, so you can't stand on it and feel secure. One solution is to first lay drop cloths along the roof next to the side of the dormer. Then, lean an extension ladder against the side of the house. Climb up and place the other half of the extension ladder or stepladder on the roof so that it lies flat, next to the dormer, and its feet rest against the top of the extension ladder. You can work off this ladder. As long as a helper holds the bottom ladder solidly, the ladder section you're on cannot slide down. If you have no helper, use masonry blocks or tie the ladder solidly so it cannot move. You can also get access to a dormer using a ladder that comes with hooks at the top to hook onto the ridge of the roof.

Staining above a Porch

Another difficult spot to stain is above a porch or an overhang of some sort. A good solution here is to cover the porch roof or overhang with drop cloths and to stand on the overhang, working off it. If you can't reach the very top of the siding, just lay a closed stepladder against the wall, using it as a small extension ladder.

Staining a Peak

The top of a roof peak is another difficult spot to stain. You may have no way to rig a ladder so that you can stain this spot safely. In this instance, use a brush clamped into a brush holder. This tool enables you to get into virtually any area of a house. The brush holder can be angled and locked in position with thumbscrews as needed.

Staining Trim

Many people like gloss or semigloss on trim, and because solid-color stain comes only in a flat finish, they use paint. Here is a good procedure for applying both materials:

First, dip the brush about one-third of the way into the paint, tap off any excess paint on the inside of the can, then apply it, brushing it out. Paint from the dry into the wet: Start each succeeding brushful of paint about 12" (30.5 cm) away from the last brushful, and paint back toward it.

Use enough paint or stain. If you keep dipping the brush in one-third of the way, you will not have a problem. Avoid excessive brushing; apply the paint, let it set up for a moment, then dry-brush it—draw an empty brush across it to smooth it out. Every now and then check the trim for sags and brush these out. As you go, some drips are sure to fall on the adjacent siding. Wipe them off immediately with a rag moistened in paint thinner (either water or mineral spirits, depending on the base of your stain or paint).

LEFT **Solid-color stain can be applied to clapboard with a pad, brush, roller, or by spray.**

Painting and Staining Windows

I cannot tell you how many times I have seen numbered sequences for painting the parts of doors and windows in a certain order. To me, this is overkill. Just remember the following points.

Paint or apply solid-color stain to a window from the inside out. That is, open the window a few inches on the top and bottom and paint it; then open both halves (assuming it is a double-hung window) so that you can paint the portions of the rails that are exposed.

When the windows themselves are finished, paint the frame, again using the dry-into-wet method. When the window is finished, take a careful look at it. Check for any missed spots or sags in the paint or stain. Use the tip of the brush to brush them out. Be particularly mindful of the window sill—paint can run down over the window and collect there.

Staining Doors

To stain or paint a door, open it completely, first being sure that a clean, dust-free drop cloth is pulled underneath to protect the floor and walls from spatters. How you paint depends on whether the door is paneled or flush, but the key concept, as with trim, is the laying off. Apply the paint and then brush it out smoothly with a dry brush.

On a flush door, dip the brush about 1" (2.5 cm) into the paint, tap off any excess paint on the inside of the can, and paint the hinge edge of the door with sweeping strokes. After you apply the paint, bring your dry brush across it with upward strokes.

Get in the habit of checking for sags a few minutes after you apply the paint and brush these out with gentle laying-off strokes.

When you are painting a narrow edge, do not push the brush against it so hard that the brush touches the sides. Doing so can lead to a brush malady called fingering—clumps of bristles that are separated—which will ruin the brush.

Paint the other edge, then the face of the door. Do it in quarters, first applying the paint horizontally, and then vertically, and finally laying it off with light, upward strokes. Paint an adjacent quarter the same way, then the bottom quarters, making your final laying-off strokes overlap the previously applied paint.

If you are coating a paneled door, first paint the edges, and then paint from the inside out: the perimeters of the panels followed by the rails, then the stiles.

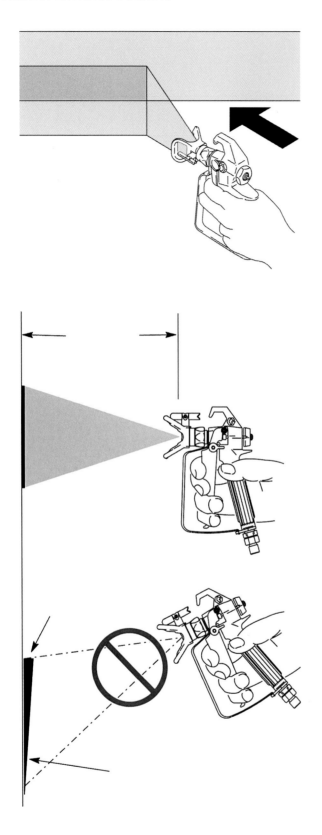

LEFT **It's best to apply stain in overlapping bands. The gun should be aimed to overlap each stroke by half. Of course, after the spray is applied, it's necessary to backbrush it.**

ABOVE **Hold the spray gun so it is parallel to the surface. If the spray gun is tilted downward or upward, you will produce an uneven finish. If you swing the gun as you spray, certain areas will be more heavily covered than others.**

Spraying

The best way to apply paint or stain from a spray gun is to make overlapping patterns, much as you would when mowing a lawn. To spray a flat surface, such as plywood walls or asbestos cement shingles, apply a band of spray, then another that slightly overlaps the first. Try to limit the degree of overlap—all you need is enough to close any gaps between bands. Too much overlap can result in too large a stain buildup.

When spraying, position your body parallel to the surface being painted and keep the gun parallel to the surface as you go. Hold it 6" to 8" (15.2 cm to 20.3 cm) from the surface. A common error is to apply the stain in sweeping arcs. This method results in a buildup of stain that's heavier in the middle and thinner at the edges.

Each time you turn off the gun and start a new band, have the gun moving before you turn it on. Doing so avoids a heavier buildup of stain where you start compared to other areas.Use the same technique at the end of the stroke. Turn off the gun while your arm is moving. If you stop moving the gun, you will get a big stain buildup.

Spraying, of course, is not only for flat surfaces. The average job also calls for the spraying of inside and outside corners. To spray an inside corner, hold the gun 6" to 8" (15.2 cm to 20.3 cm) from the corner. Then just move the gun. The spray overlaps the corner, but no excessive paint buildup will result. Remember to have the gun moving before you turn it on, both before and after the strokes.

To spray outside corners, also locate the gun 6" to 8" (15.2 cm to 20.3 cm) from the corner. Turn the gun 90°, and then spray, moving the gun along vertically. As you do, the spray pattern overlaps both of the walls that are adjacent to the corner.

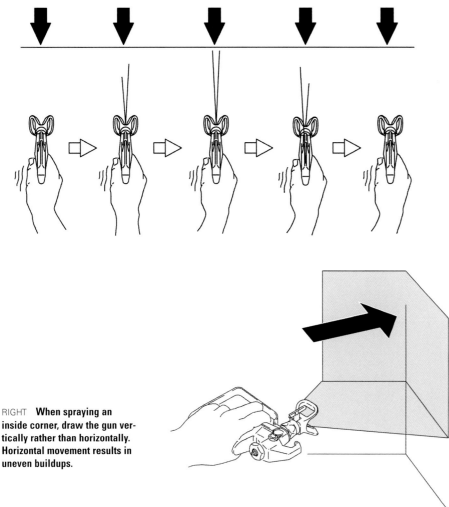

LEFT **The best way to start applying stain is to squeeze the trigger before you hit the area you want to stain, draw the gun across, and then release the trigger when you're past the area.**

RIGHT **When spraying an inside corner, draw the gun vertically rather than horizontally. Horizontal movement results in uneven buildups.**

Spraying Clapboard and Other Lap Siding

If you are staining clapboard or other siding that overlaps, it is best to do it in a few steps. Keeping in mind the advice to keep the spray gun moving, paint the bottoms of the courses first, then move across the face of the boards. Backbrush as you go (or let a helper do it).

If you are painting rough surfaces, spray the bottom of the courses, then the faces. Rougher surfaces are less likely to need backbrushing—at least for the first coat—than smooth surfaces.

When you are using stain, spray on the material, and then backbrush it into the surface. A spray wand is helpful for reaching out-of-the-way places and for keeping the spray parallel to the surface. When spraying siding, hit between courses first, then spray the faces.

> **Tip:** If there is the slightest wind, do not use the spray gun. Even a slight breeze can carry the stain all over the place, such as on parked cars!

Safety Measures

It is important to protect yourself when spray painting. A respirator is recommended so that you do not breathe in the fumes. Also wear goggles to protect your eyes. (The wraparound kind are best for staining or painting.) A pair of cotton gloves and a long-sleeved shirt is needed, too. Wear clothes that you do not mind discarding when the job is done. Alternatively, you can use disposable coveralls, which are inexpensive and lightweight.

ABOVE **Many sheds are built with Texture 1-11, a siding characterized by a rough surface. A fluffy, napped pad applicator, as shown here, usually works well for this and for similar rough woods.**

> Safeguarding Tools

At times during any staining job, you will stop for a break or lunch. It is a good idea to safeguard tools when you take a break. To keep the roller brush or paint pad wet, immerse it in the stain or paint can and put the can in the shade. You can also wrap the tool in plastic wrap. It is not a good idea to put a brush in a can because it puts stress on the bristles and could deform them. Just wrap it airtight in plastic and lay it on its side. Follow the manufacturer's directions for handling spray equipment.

Sheds

Staining a shed is not really any different than staining a house, except it is usually easier to do because the do-it-yourselfer can reach all areas on the shed without having to use an extension ladder. However, keep in mind the following elements of the job.

Using the Correct Color

Make sure that the colors that you use on the shed harmonize with the color of the house. A shed can be a different color, but it should be in the same family of colors as the house or relate to one of the trim or accent colors.

Many people stain (or paint) a shed with the same colors used on a house. If the house, say, has dark brown trim and light brown siding, so does the shed. The big idea in staining a shed is not to make it stand out. The buildings should look harmonious.

Repairs

Shed repairs can be performed in the same way as they are on the siding of a home. See chapter three for details on making repairs.

Sometimes, the hardware on a shed may get rusty or corroded. Your best bet is to simply replace the pieces using corrosion-resistant stainless-steel or high-quality galvanized hardware.

Like a house, a shed can be stained using a sprayer, a brush, a roller, or pad. It's best, as with a house, to do the siding first, the finish with the trim. Follow the same techniques with the shed as you would with a house.

Here are some additional tips for staining a shed:
- Make repairs as necessary.
- Place drop cloths on the ground around the shed.
- Start the job with the siding.
- If you are applying a penetrating stain, apply the material with a brush, sprayer, or pad, starting from the top of the shed and working your way down.
- As you apply the stain, use a brush or pad to brush it out.
- When the siding portion is done, paint or stain the trim.

BELOW   **Shown is a typical shed, coated with a
clear stain. Access to siding adjacent to close trees
and shrubs is easier in late fall or early spring.**

Staining Log Houses

Log houses are particularly susceptible to decay because of the deep notches in large logs. These notches allow moisture to penetrate the wood, and moisture, of course, is what decay needs to form.

Logs are also particularly susceptible to decay because the end of the logs is exposed excessively, particularly at the corners of the structure. The exposure of this end grain, plus the notching of the logs, allows for easy water penetration. Properly constructing a log home—meaning having the proper size overhangs—as well as applying a penetrating stain reduces the development of decay.

Aesthetically, because of their rustic appearance, penetrating finishes are much better to use on log cabins than film-forming finishes such as paint and solid-color stain.

Clear stains with preservatives weather to light brown or tan. The coating also prevents decay, assuming that the house has been made properly. Note that deep surface cracks, the lower courses of logs, the corners of the structure, and the bottom of windows and doors often trap moisture and are particularly vulnerable to decay. Hence, it is important to keep these areas well protected.

You can also use oil-based, semitransparent stains, which, indeed, last longer than clear coatings, just as they do on other wood. If a log structure is weathered, the application of stain can prevent further deterioration of the wood.

Staining Wooden Roofs

A wooden roof should never be left uncoated, because it will inevitably be attacked by sun and water. Rain or snow that falls on an uncoated roof will be absorbed. Also, moisture from various sources, such as showers, may come from the inside of the house, resulting in shingles or shakes that expand and contract and eventually crack.

It's a bad idea to use either paint or solid-color stain or varnish on a roof. If you do, the moisture that gathers inside the roofing will drive up and out, and push the finish off the shingles or shakes. What's

> Treating Logs with Borates

Log structures with moisture problems can also be treated with borates. The material is manufactured for brush or spray application or as a "rod" that can be inserted in $\frac{1}{4}$" (0.6 cm) holes drilled into the wood, and then plugged with pieces of dowel saturated with preservative. The material diffuses through wet wood and provides protection against decay and wood-destroying insects. Because the borates eventually leach from the wood, pretreatment is usually necessary and is usually applied by pest-control operators, log cabin manufacturers, and pole treaters.

If the logs or sections of logs are decayed, these pieces should be removed and replaced with new wood. Borates are particularly useful where the problem wood is hard to reach.

> Better Drying

Before and during the nineteenth century, wood shingles were commonly used on roofs and were fastened to widely spaced nailing strips without the use of tarred or asphalt felts as a secondary barrier to moisture. Today, asphalt is used so wood shingles typically dry less quickly. Providing an airspace between the shingle and the felt covering vastly improves drying times. This can be achieved by securing furring strips (1' x 2' [30.5 cm x 61 cm] boards) to the felted roof decks. The strips should be parallel to the trusses or rafters. Then attach widely spaced nailers perpendicular to the furring strips. When water gets past the shingles, it drains away. As of this writing, a product called "Cedar Breather," is available. It is a thick plastic mesh that can be applied on the roofing felt deck to create some degree of airspace between the shingles and the felt-covered shingles.

OPPOSITE TOP **The end grain of a log home in most vulnerable to water penetration, so it is important to make sure it is well coated.**

OPPOSITE BOTTOM
Penetrating finishes are the way to go with log homes. Here, a clear penetrating stain has been used, and should be periodically recoated (every year or so).

more, the moisture that's inside the wood can encourage decay, which can destroy the roof itself.

Siding is not subject to the same problems that roofing is because it is not assaulted by water in the same way. On the other hand, it too, must be protected with some sort of coating.

The best coating for a roof is a penetrating semitransparent stain with a preservative. If you are installing a new wooden roof, the best way to coat it is to apply the finish on the back of the shingles or shakes as well as on the sides or end grain.

One way to coat the shakes is to dip them into a bucket that coats two-thirds of their length, leaving the one-third that will not be exposed to the weather uncoated. Then stand them vertically until the finish has dried. Any additional coats can be applied by brushing or spraying after the shingles have been installed. If the backs of the shingles can't be finished (they've been installed), remember that water may

get under the shingles and cause more curling than otherwise would take place. If you use a light-colored finish, also note that tannins may seep out of the wood if it's a bleeding type (cedar or redwood).

Maintenance

It's a good idea to maintain a roof. Leaves and other debris often accumulate in roof valleys, which will trap moisture and increases the likelihood of decay. Remove this debris and any overhanging tree limbs or vines that block the sun extensively.

Also check the roof for moss or lichen growth. The single most effective way to prevent moss from developing on roofs is to use a zinc, steel, or copper ridge cap. The normal corrosion from these metals washes down and protects the wood.

Finishing for the Day

When you are finished for the day, you must follow some basic finishing steps. First, take down ladders if they are in such a position on the house that someone could accidentally walk into them or if they are located where children play.

You should also stop applying coating at a structural break in the house, say, at the end of a wall or up to the edge of an addition. Avoid stopping midway through staining a wall; when you pick up the next day, your strokes of freshly applied stain will overlap the existing dry coat and leave a lapmark.

Cleaning Brushes, Pads, and Rollers

To clean stain or paint applicators properly, you must remove as much of the stain as you can before cleaning with solvents. For brushes, you can proceed as follows. Lay the brush on a sheet of newspaper, and then push down on the bristles with a scraper or joint compound knife, squeezing out as much stain as possible.

When you have removed as much stain as possible from the brush, the next step is to wash it. If the brush was used with water-based stain, immerse the

> Good Points to Remember

- As with other staining jobs, work in the shade. It's better for the person and avoids quick drying of stain, which can lead to lapmarks.

- Work in small sections so you can easily control the application.

- Cover up as much as you can before you begin.

- Be particularly careful when covering screens. Stain or paint can be very difficult to remove from them.

- When securing plastic over windows and other painted or stained trim, use painter's tape rather than masking tape.

- The roller is an excellent tool to use with solid-color stain.

- To stain the dormers and other roof protrusions, laying half of an extension ladder on the roof makes for a handy way to get access.

- When painting (or using solid-color stain), use the dry-into-the-wet

method. Apply paint about a foot away from last wet edge and paint back toward the edge.

- After staining or painting a section, draw your undipped applicator over the area to smooth out and remove excess material.

- When spraying, keep the sprayer level and parallel to the surface.

- If using an airless spray, make sure you don't let the spray hit your flesh. The sprayer is powerful enough to cut you.

- End grain on a log house is particularly vulnerable for water penetration. Make sure it's well coated.

- Semitransparent oil-based stain is a good material for coating a roof.

- Make sure debris is kept off roofs, and cut back trees that provide excessive shade. These things can lead to moisture problems—and rot.

OPPOSITE **A house with cedar shingle roof coated with semi-transparent oil-based stain. Wooden roofs are beautiful, but require more maintenance compared to other types of roof material.**

bristles in a solution of water and mild soap. Knead the bristles with your hand, then rinse in clear, running water. Mount the brush on a spinning tool, if you have one, and spin it inside a large box so the liquid from the brush does not fly all over the place. Wrap the brush in newspaper or in its original package or its "keeper," and hang it up. If you don't have a spinning tool, put the brush in a plastic or paper bag, then grab the handle and shake the stain out of the bristles.

If the brush was used with oil-based stain, follow the previous procedure to remove as much stain as

possible, then immerse the bristles in a can of mineral spirits, kneading them with your fingers. (You can wear rubber gloves if you wish.) Then immerse it in another can containing paint thinner and repeat the process. Next, immerse the brush in thinner again and wash. As a final step, use the spinning tool.

CHAPTER 7

Staining Furniture, Play Equipment, Fencing, and Concrete

In addition to homes, decks, and sheds, there are several other items that benefit from a perfect stain treatment: play equipment, furniture, fencing, and concrete. This chapter details how to make these jobs easier and more successful.

While you can use the same array of applicators on these items as you do on others, there are special procedures that may help. For example, while doing furniture with a brush is fine, doing a long stockade fence would be tedious, so you should think about spraying it or using a roller followed by backbrushing.

Concrete stain, which many people know nothing about, is another good stain option. It is like solid-color stain for wood in that it ends up as a film, and one of its benefits is that it is less likely to peel than paint. It can be used underfoot anywhere around the house.

OPPOSITE **Following the steps outlined in this book will make your job achievable. Most importantly, take time to relax and enjoy the fruits of your labor. Give yourself a pat on the back!**

Protecting Outdoor Equipment

Moisture is the number-one factor is creating decay, so try to keep outdoor items as dry as possible. Items that are dry will not develop decay, unless the legs of the item are in direct contact with the ground, which does harbor moisture and can be drawn up into the particular piece.

The sun can also give your finish a shorter life, so keep items out of the sun if possible when not in use. If the items are transportable, you can store them somewhere where they'll be protected from the weather. Cover large, immovable objects with tarpaulins when they aren't being used. Home improvement centers sell blue tarps, which do quite a good job.

If you can, during cold or winter seasons when the items aren't being used, move them to a garage or shed, where they will shielded from harsh environmental conditions.

Safety Concerns and Precautionary Measures

You should be aware of a number of safety concerns when coating outdoor furniture, play equipment, and fencing. One issue that has arisen in recent years is over pressure-treated wood. For years, there have been questions on the safety of this material, and recently the U.S. government banned its use in residential situations, with the ban going into effect in December 2003. Use of this wood is also limited by the European Union.

The problem is how the pressure-treated material, also known as CCA (for chromated copper arsenates), is made. The goal in making it was to provide protection against insects, fungi, and rot, which can destroy wood, particularly wood in direct contact with the soil. To achieve this, manufacturers pressure-injected a certain amount of arsenic into the wood to produce a product that lasted ten times longer than

BELOW **This cedar bench, finished with a semitransparent stain, will be protected for three or more years. The color fits the environment well.**

OPPOSITE **This furniture was given two coats of white, solid-color stain. The finish is unlikely to peel, but it can.**

untreated wood. The wood generally has a greenish or brownish appearance.

The problem is threefold. First, it is suspected that the chromium arsenic in the wood can leach out when handled, getting on skin and then inside the body when fingers are touched to lips or go inside the mouth. Various studies have pointed to an increased risk of certain cancers after long-term exposure, though it is still a topic of intense debate. The second problem is when the material is cut. Sawing produces sawdust, which can be inhaled, intensifying the potential for exposure. A third problem is the burning of treated wood, which leads to the formation of a smoke that contains the toxic chemicals.

Many experts advise tearing out the material and discarding it. Another solution is to stain or paint the material to lock in the arsenic. The stain or paint acts as a protective barrier between the wood and skin.

Both penetrating stain and paint can do this job quite well. Whatever you apply, make sure that the coating doesn't wear off (such as with contact). Be aware that the finish can wear away. If you use a clear finish, plan on recoating every year. If a semitransparent stain is used, recoat every two or three years. The advantage of these types of stain is, again, that they don't peel. You can also use paint or solid-color stain, but these materials may peel, the former much more likely than the latter.

> Tip: Applying Stain to CCA-treated Wood

In your zeal to lock poison in, you may be tempted to overapply the stain. You don't have to, and doing so can lead to other problems, such as the stain not drying properly or you end up with a sticky mess.

Another safety concern unrelated to CCA is mildewcides. If you are going to coat tables where food and drink are going to be served, remember that some stains (and paint) contain a mildewcide to inhibit the growth of mildew. These chemicals can cause allergic or toxic reactions. After the finish has dried for about a week, it is unlikely to cause an allergic reaction. However, food should never be placed in direct contact with a stain containing a mildewcide.

Staining Furniture

In terms of applying a stain to furniture, you can use a brush, roller, or spray—whatever the manufacturer suggests. Again, the brush is the preferred applicator because you can drive the stain deeper into the surface.

If the piece if movable, move it on to a drop cloth in a shady spot, if available. Following the manufacturer's recommendations for the amount to use, and begin applying the stain.

If the piece has narrow areas, you may find a brush handy. If there are broad, flat areas, you can use a pad, perhaps on a stick so you can reach out-of-the-way spots. Remember to always finish the application by backbrushing, or using a dry pad to make a final swipe at the finish.

Here's a good trick: If the feet of the piece are going to be in contact with the ground, fill a can with the coating and, in turn, dip each of the leg ends in it so that the coating is well absorbed by the end grain of the wood.

You can exercise your design sense with furniture and play equipment just as you do with a house. For example, the pieces you stain needn't be finished in one color. Also, if you want to invest the time and effort, you can jazz up a piece of furniture by making part of it one color, like green, and part of it white. In

OPPOSITE **These chairs, coated with semitransparent stain, have narrow parts and were coated with a brush.**

ABOVE **These two Adirondack chairs illustrate two options for staining. For a project like this, a brush is the handiest applicator.**

> Getting the Right Color

The wrong color on a fence can be a disaster. What looks brown in the can may appear to be pumpkin-orange on the wood. To ensure you get the color you want, dab a little of the stain on the fence before you start and allow it to dry. Semitransparent stain works best for color matching.

this instance, I suggest you do one color completely, then to the other. If you don't trust yourself not to spill some of the second color onto the first color, cover vulnerable areas with painter's tape.

Staining Fencing

Depending on type, probably the best way to stain a long fence—and fences tend to be long—is with a sprayer. Using a sprayer, though, is a compromise: you will use more stain than if you use a brush, pad, or roller. If you value your time, however, it is definitely the preferred method. (See chapter six, page 100, for more information on spray equipment, as well as tips on using it.)

Before spraying, start by cleaning the fence as described in chapter three. Fences tend to get highly discolored from sun, dirt, tannins, mildew, and whatever, and a good cleaning is required. Fences are also usually long, so your best bet is to use cleanser along with a power washer—this method is easier and faster than having to scrub the wood by hand.

When cleaning is complete, lay drop cloths—preferably canvas but heavy-duty plastic is fine, too—on the ground on both sides of the fence,

assuming the fence has openings in it. You want to protect against the spray getting on the ground. You also want to protect against it floating in a cloud and getting on something else—like a car.

To prevent this from occurring, get a helper to hold a piece of $\frac{1}{4}$" x 4' x 8' (0.6 cm x 121.9 cm x 243.8 cm) light plywood so the overspray falls harmlessly against it. You can start at either end of a fence, moving it along as you do. It is also advisable for both you and your helper to wear goggles and for the helper to wear a respirator and to dress so his or her arms, legs, and head are fully covered.

Using a Brush, Roller, or Pad

You can, of course, use a brush, roller, or pad, but if you are staining something like a stockade fence, which is composed of side-by-side staves, this can take awhile. If you do use these tools, you should place drop cloths on the ground. Here are some tips on using these various tools on a stockade fence, one of the most popular kinds of fences:

• Brush—Use a 4" or 5" (10.2 cm or 20.3 cm) staining brush, whatever kind you can most easily wield.

- Process—Use a wide-mouth container. Dip the brush in halfway, and apply the stain, starting from the top of the fence and brushing toward the bottom. Do five or six boards at a time. As you approach the bottom of the fence, do not dip the brush into the stain. If you do, you may have an excessive amount of stain on your brush, which could run down the boards and pool on the ground. Try doing the bottom few inches of each board with an undipped, "dry" brush. When you finish applying the stain to one area go onto the next, but come back after the next section has stain on it and use a dry brush to thoroughly backbrush the boards.

- Pad—The best type of pad to use is one with a fluffy nap—the same nap you would use on a deck. Pads should be used with a special assembly rigged with a roller in it. Follow the general procedure as for a brush. Apply the material to five or six boards, use a dry pad to apply the stain, and then go on to the next area before going back over the first with a dry pad. Use a stick that you screw the pad onto to make the job easier on your back.

- Rollers—If you use a roller with a penetrating stain, then you should also backbrush it. If you use a roller, or any other applicator, with solid-color stain, make sure that there are no drips on the fence. If there are, brush them out. I would hesitate before using a solid-color stain on a fence. Fence stakes may be mounted in the soil, which can draw up water, which, as it pushes itself up and out, tends to make the stain peel.

Staining Concrete

Concrete stain is one of those products that most of us are aware of but few know anything about. It's very much worth knowing about because it can add pizzazz and protection to many things around the house. Theoretically, you can use it on raw concrete and previously painted surfaces, but think of it for uncoated concrete only. Preparation of previously painted surfaces may include stripping, a monumental task. Think also of concrete stain for flat surfaces, including patios, steps, walls, driveways, garages, even around the pool area. If you have raw vertical surfaces to do, such as a foundation wall, latex paint is best. Concrete stain is meant for places that are to be walked on.

Just what is concrete stain? For one thing, like solid-color stain for wood, it's not really a penetrating stain. It does penetrate a bit, but it basically forms a film, albeit a thin one, that's thinner than a paint film, just like solid-color stain does. It is basically an acrylic

ABOVE **What you see here is not atypical of how discolored and dirty fences can get. This blemish is a blend of mildew, dirt, and tannin extractives. If you have access to a power washer, that's the best way to go.**

ABOVE **After a thorough cleaning, a pad on a stick is used to apply the stain. The best tool to use, however, is a spray gun followed by back-brushing because there is a large surface area.**

LEFT **Here, a semitransparent oil-based stain has been used on this fence. It blends in beautifully with the foliage and flowers.**

product—also like a solid-color stain. If the surface is prepared properly it usually will not come off, which is saying a lot when you consider that one of the places it can be used is the driveway.

It is available in flat finish only. Because of its thinness, it allows the graininess of concrete to show through, which can be helpful for creating better friction underfoot. Paint is thicker and does not allow for the same degree of friction.

Preparation

The key to success with concrete stain, as with so many other coatings tasks, is in preparation and, of course, following the manufacturer's instructions on the label.

No new concrete should be coated until ninety days after it has been poured. Why? It leaches alkalis, which can interfere with the adhesion of the coating.

Raw Concrete

The first step in preparing concrete for staining is to clean the surface. Use a broom to sweep the floor clean or a shop vacuum or an air compressor to blow off grit and dirt. If you use the latter, you must wear safety goggles.

Any stains on the floor must come up. Grease stains are usually relatively easy to remove. First, use a putty knife to scrape up any grease deposits. Then use a heavy-duty solution of water and cleaner or degreaser to remove the stains that are left, scrubbing as needed and rinsing carefully. Stain does not adhere to grease, no matter how small the spot. If

OPPOSITE **Here, paint was used to coat the railing around the deck. Its chances of peeling are lessened because it's not in direct contact with the ground, which contains moisture.**

the grease does not come up when the degreaser is diluted with water, it may be necessary to use the cleaner full-strength.

Oil Stains

Oil stains are worse than grease stains because oil penetrates into concrete, and the longer it stays, the more deeply it penetrates. Hence, to remove it, you need something that also penetrates.

Soak up as much surface oil as you can with a rag. Resist the temptation to wipe—the result will be a bigger stain, and the oil will be driven deeper into the concrete. Once you have finished with the rag, dispose of it by sealing it in a 1-gallon (3.8-liter) can filled with water; oil-soaked rags can spontaneously burst into flames.

To remove the rest of the oil, you have a couple of options. You can purchase a powdered floor-drying material at a local automotive supply store; or you can sprinkle portland cement on the stain, allow it to stay on the stain for twenty-four hours, and then sweep it up. Repeat the procedure until all the stain is gone. Another option is to purchase a commercial cleaner.

Rust Stains

A rust stain is not true rust; it does not keep growing, as rust does. If you are staining it, just cover the stain with a coat of concrete primer. However, you can also remove the stain, if you wish. The material to use here is the same thing you use on wood—oxalic acid, which is part of many wood-cleaning solutions.

Etching the Concrete

It is crucial to etch new concrete—roughen it so the coatings adhere better. A number of companies make this product. In fact, companies that manufacturer concrete stain ordinarily offer an etcher as well.

> Don't Stain Stucco

Although stucco is a concrete product, you should not stain (or paint) it, because unpainted or unstained stucco can last for years. Painted stucco requires periodic recoating. Just clean it with hot water and detergent and a rough nylon-bristle brush.

Once the soil is removed, the stucco may be clean and bright—it will not need repainting. In some instances you will also find mildew, efflorescence, and peeling paint. Peeling paint can be removed with a wire brush. It is not a good idea to power wash stucco heavily because you can knock down its texture. However, there is nothing wrong with a light washing. If there are gaps in the stucco, patch them with an acrylic latex caulk.

Concrete Patches

Concrete may have gaps or holes in it, which must be repaired before any staining is done. You can use concrete patcher for this job. It is a good idea to allow at least thirty days to pass before you stain these patches, to make sure that they have given up all the alkalis.

Staining the Concrete

Variations exist in the directions from manufacturer to manufacturer for applying concrete stain, but here is the general procedure:

After cleaning and etching, apply a primer and allow it to cure for eight hours or so. Then apply the stain with either a $\frac{1}{4}$"- or $\frac{3}{8}$"- (0.6-cm or 1-cm) roller or a nylon/polyester brush.

It is important to stir the stain frequently. If you are using more than one gallon (3.8 liter), pour all the gallons in a five-gallon (19 liter) container and box them—pour the stain back and forth between the gallons and

OPPOSITE **Concrete stain allows you to add pizzazz underfoot. For vertical surfaces, it's best to use latex stains or paints.**

five-gallon container—to make sure the color is uniform throughout.

The idea when applying concrete stain, just as it is with wood, is to apply it at the rate that the manufacturer suggests, which is usually 400 to 600 square feet (37.2 to 55.7 square meters) per gallon. Applying too much can lead to peeling. The stain adheres to the surface because it bonds to the primer, which acts as a sort of flat sheet of adhesive. Once dry, the bond is quite strong.

As you apply the stain, smooth it out by rolling an undipped roller across it with long, even strokes in one direction. You may find the job easier if you attach the roller to a pole so you don't have to bend over so much.

Concrete varies in porosity, so you might have to apply two coats to get the uniform color you want. Concrete stains are available in custom colors. Give the dealer the sample of the color you want and he or she will make it. Pay particular attention to what manufacturers say about drying time required before walking or driving on the stain. For example, Behr suggest you wait seventy-two hours before driving on the surface.

> Good Points to Remember

- If furniture or playground equipment is made of CCA (pressure-treated) wood, it is important to keep it well coated so the wood, which contains arsenic, does not come in contact with skin or food.

- As with other wooden items, it's important not to overapply the coating.

- A good trick for saturating furniture or play equipment ends that will come into contact with the ground—and can suck moisture up from it—is to dip them into a container half-filled with the coating, thereby ensuring that the feet are well coated.

- Moisture is the number-one enemy of furniture or playground equipment. If you have an opportunity for storing these items so they're protected from water (such as under a porch), by all means do so. You can also cover them with tarps.

- Any coating containing a mildewcide (check the label or call the manufacturer's 800 number) can cause allergic or toxic reactions.

- Fencing in direct contact with the ground is the most vulnerable to decay.

- Soaking ground-contact fence parts in stain is a good idea.

- A power washer is a convenient tool for cleaning a fence.

- Sprayers work well for coating a fence. Use plywood as a backup so stain doesn't float in the air—and onto someplace where it's not supposed to be.

- Don't overapply stain. Follow the manufacturer's recommendations.

- Allow concrete to cure before staining it.

- Don't walk or drive on stain until after the time periods specified by manufacturer has passed.

Glossary and Tips

A glossary of terms used in the text as well as terms and tips not included to increase your knowledge of staining and painting follows:

Acrylic—A high-quality synthetic binder, which is a chemical that glues chemical particles together while in suspension and adds considerably to a paint's or stain's wearability and color retention.

Additives—Chemicals that are added to paint or stain formulations to impart various desirable characteristics, such as mildew resistance, low spatter, and little or no foaming.

Adhesion—The ability of dried paint or solid-color stain to remain on the surface. Wet adhesion occurs when paint adheres to a surface despite its being wet. Latex paint and solid-color stain are prime examples, as are some waterproofing paints. They can be applied when a surface is actually wet from dew rain, though there is a point at which they will run. Painters describe adhesion with the term bonding.

Airless sprayer—Machine used to spray paint or stain. It uses a pump to atomize the paint. It puts out more stain than any other type of sprayer.

Algae—Brownish or reddish aquatic plants that normally grow in areas of a house or building that are sheltered from the sun.

Alligatoring—Form of paint or stain failure in which the paint or stain cracks apart and resembles the hide of an alligator. It is one of the more common forms of paint or stain failure. Essentially, the paint is not adhering for one reason or another. When this occurs, the film lifts off the surface, and the stress cracks it. Left alone, the paint gradually peels.

Aromatic oils—Oils present in some woods, such as cypress, teak, and the cedars (except western red cedar), that can cause finishing problems. They can slow down drying of coatings, leaving them sticky, and often cause blistering, softening, wrinkling, and general disintegration. This problem is caused mainly by the way the wood was kiln-dried.

Backbrushing—Process of brushing out a material applied with another type of applicator. The classic use of backbrushing occurs when stain or clear finish is applied to raw wood, stain or clear coating with a pump sprayer. Without back-brushing, the material may lie on the surface, ultimately drying into a sticky puddle and then to a hard film, which can peel. Backbrushing avoids this, because the action of the brush drives the product deep into the wood pores. In a word, they penetrate deeply into the wood and, therefore, cannot peel. Backbrushing is also commonly done after spraying. The spray gets the stain (or paint) onto the surface, and the brush is used to smooth it out.

Backrolling—Same thing as backbrushing except a roller is used. The classic use is on walls. The paint is applied with a roller, the next strip is done, and then the painter comes back and rolls over—backrolls—the applied paint with a relatively dry roller to smooth it out. Backrolling is used in any situation where the paint is thickly applied.

Batch code—Method of identifying when and where a particular paint or stain was made to ensure color consistency.

Blisters—In exterior painting, an expanded part of a paint or solid-color stain; the stage before cracking and peeling. Blisters occur for many reasons, but one of the main ones is that water vapor, migrating from inside the house, gets trapped behind the film. As the vapor pushes outward, the paint film is pushed and lifted off the surface, forming a blister. You can confirm the reason by puncturing the blister and seeing if water runs out.

Boxing—Mixing paint or stain by pouring it back and forth between containers. It is the best nonmechanical way to mix paint.

Breathing—The ability of paint or stain to allow moisture vapor to pass harmlessly through a coating without damaging it. Latex paint or stain, for example, breathes whereas oil-based paint does not, making the latter more likely to peel.

Bristles—Fibers of hair that constitute the working end of a brush. Bristle is a term that is sometimes misunderstood. It used to refer to a bristle brush, which implies that the brush is a China, or natural-bristle, brush. At other times it is used to describe the bristles on a synthetic brush. Today, the term must be seen in context to determine its meaning.

Caulk—Flexible material used to fill the seams or joints of a house. It is applied wherever dissimilar materials meet, such as masonry and wood, and where windows, doors, and the like meet. Buildings expand and contract; without a flexible material to seal these seams, water, cold, and heat can pass in and out of the house easily, affecting heating and cooling and leading to much higher fuel costs. Caulk comes in a variety of types, but essentially it is designed for either interior use, in which case it is mildew-resistant, or for exterior use.

Chalking—Surface of paint film turning to a powder. This occurs when the binder in the paint cannot stand up to the weather conditions.

Clear stain—Clear, penetrating stain that seeps into the pores of wood to protect it against water intrusion. The clear stain can also protect against the sun if it has a protective agent in it and against fungi and insects if it contains a preservative.

Color chip—Small square of color found in paint brochures. Chips are actually made of paint so you can get an idea of what the true color is. The gloss or sheen of the paint is also accurately depicted.

Color retention—The ability of paint or stain to hold its color without fading.

Coverage—Area that a paint covers and/or how well it covers. The standard coverage figure given will depends on which applicator is used. Brushes use the least amount of stain or paint, and rollers the most. Color also is a factor.

Crawling—Adhesion problem in which paint is incompatible with substrate and beads up or otherwise does not penetrate, such as oil on wax.

Cupping—A distortion or twist across the flatness of a board. Wide boards cup more than narrow boards. Boards can also twist from one to the other, deviating from a straight line along the length of the piece; this is also known as a crook.

Cutting in—Using a brush to apply a different color or gloss (or both) of paint to another area without getting any of the new material where it does not belong. Painters speak of cutting in the molding or windows, or the line where the wall paint meets the ceiling paint.

Drops—Short for drop cloths, the painter's cloths used to protect areas from paint. Drop cloths come in a variety of sizes, but usually 9' by 12' (2.7 m x 3.7 m), and in various textures. Although the average drop cloth is not waterproof, it will absorb drops of paint. Drop cloths may also be plastic.

Eggshell—The sheen level of a paint that is roughly that of an eggshell, also known as satin flat.

Emulsion—Coating mixture in which oil and water are compatible.

Enamel—Generally, a hard, shiny paint. The term is confusing because it also is applied to flat paints. Enamel originally referred to a shiny, oil-based paint.

Etch—Washing of a surface with acid to roughen it and provide better tooth for primer or paint.

Extractives—Substances in wood that affect its properties. Depending on the species, wood may contain water-soluble extractives, such as tannins, pitch, or oil. Each of these substances has its own properties and characteristics. Although they involve only a small percentage of the wood, they are disproportionately important in terms of their effect on a number of wood properties, including color, decay and insect resistance, odor, permeability, density, and hardness. Without extractives, pitch, and oil, many woods would appear essentially identical except for their anatomical features.

Water-soluble extractives are located in the cells in the heartwoods of both hardwoods and softwoods. They are particularly plentiful in woods used outdoors, such as western red cedar, redwood, and cypress, and are found in lesser amounts in Douglas fir and southern yellow pine where heartwood is present. The handsome color, dimensional stability, and decay resistance of many species are due to extractives. However, these extractives can interfere with finishing, both when the finish is applied and later. Because they are water-soluble, water that saturates the woods seeps down and solubilizes them. They then leech to the surface and stain it a reddish brown, something particularly noticeable with white or light-colored paints or solid-colored stains.

Fading—Loss of color due to weather, time, and/or light.

Feathering—Technique that describes the smoothing of a patching material so that the outer edges blend into nothingness. Also, the brush application of paint or stain where one brushful of paint, by lifting the last part of the stroke, is blended seamlessly into an adjacent wet edge.

Film forming—Refers to stains (as well as paint) that dry into a microscopically thin film that is both opaque and subject to peeling.

Flat—Paint or stain without any sheen.

Glazing compound—The correct name for window putty, used for sealing around panes of glass.

Gloss—The amount of shine in a finish. Gloss paint refers to very shiny paint. A device called a gloss meter is used to measure the glossiness. On the meter the maximum gloss is 69 to 70 degrees, and this surface is like glass. One step down is semigloss, which is 35 on the meter. Below this is eggshell, 20 to 35; and the lowest gloss of all, flat, is below 15. The numbers are arrived at by focusing a specified amount of light onto a surface and then measuring it. Note that one manufacturer may call a paint high-gloss, but according to objective measurements it may be less or more than other manufacturers' high-gloss paints. In other words, one company's semigloss may be another company's gloss.

Grain raising—Swelling or raising of wood grain in raw wood due to the absorption of water or other solvents.

Heartwood and sapwood—A dark column of wood (heartwood) and the lighter column of wood that surrounds it (sapwood). The sapwood is composed of live cells that carry water and nutrients from the roots to the leaves and that provide mechanical support. The heartwood, which is composed of dead cells, provides only mechanical support.

The heartwood, being already dead, provides a much better resistance to decay than sapwood. Some species, such as southern yellow pine, have a much wider sapwood zone than other species, such as cedar and redwood and, therefore, much less decay resistance.

Old or original-growth timber from some species, such as cypress, is notable for its natural resistance to decay and insects. Second-growth lumber contains a much larger amount of sapwood than old-growth lumber and is much more susceptible to decay than old-growth; its heartwood is not as resistant to decay as old-growth heartwood.

Hide—The ability of paint or stain to obscure the color of the stain or paint to which it has been applied. The hide is provided by the prime pigment in the stain or paint. For example, in good-quality white or pastel paints, titanium dioxide is the prime pigment.

Holiday—Slang for a missed spot when painting or staining. The term first surfaced many years ago in regard to applying tar to a boat; a missed spot was called a holiday or vacation, in the sense that it fills a gap in the routine. Painters say that holidays are much more likely to occur when painting (or staining) is done at night than in the day; natural light is much better.

HVLP sprayer—Stands for high-volume, low-pressure. This sprayer sprays paint or stain using very little pressure, which gives you greater control of the spray. Most painters do not use it outside because it's too slow.

Knots—Irregularities in wood growth. The presence of knots affects the ability to paint lumber and is generally a function of lumber grade. Knots are mostly exposed on the end grain of wood. End-grained wood absorbs more finish than flat- or edge-grained lumber, which affects the way the paint looks. In pine, knots often contain a high percentage of resin, which may cause the paint above the knot to discolor. Furthermore, large knots usually crack, and a noticeable split or defect occurs. In sum, the higher grades of lumber are better to use for finishing.

Lapmark—Unsightly mark in paint or stain finish caused by applying wet paint or stain over a dry edge of paint or stain.

Latex—Emulsion of synthetic resins, commonly used to describe paint or stain that uses water as the solvent but, in fact, is not latex in the strictest sense. When latex paint was first formulated before World War II, latex came from the rubber tree and was used as a binder for the paint. When the war started, latex became scarce and synthetics were developed, but the name stuck.

Linseed oil—Vegetable oil obtained by crushing seeds of the flax plant; a basic component of some paints, chiefly the oil-based type. Raw linseed oil is available in two forms: boiled and not. Boiled means it is heated by chemical dryers (years ago it was actually cooked) so that it dries more quickly. Linseed oil is bad to put on a house—mildew love it.

Low luster—A low sheen. Note that what is low-luster paint to one manufacturer is not to another, and vice versa. It is best to check the color chip cards of manufacturers. These show just what the luster is because they are made of paint and are not photographically reproduced.

Mildew—A living organism that forms on and discolors stain and paint.

Mildewcide—Chemical agent added to or formulated into paint that kills mildew.

Oil-based paint—Any paint that thins and cleans up with mineral spirits.

Open time—The amount of time a coating stays workable or wet after it has been applied. Working in the shade can keep paint and stain, as well as stripper, wetter longer.

Painter's tape—Tape that comes in a variety of widths and lengths and somewhat resembles masking tape (although some is white and blue), though it differs greatly. Painter's tape is designed to be able to be peeled off of a surface without damaging it. Try the same thing with masking tape, and you will tear the paint or wallpaper.

Painting pad—Type of applicator used to apply paint or stain. It can be wielded by hand or with a stick attached.

Penetrating stain—Refers to stains that work by seeping down into the wood like sauce in sponge cake. (See also Film forming.)

Pigment—Main solid ingredient in paint or stain that gives the material its color and hiding power.

Pitch—In most pines and Douglas fir trees, substance exuded from either the sapwood or the heartwood. It is usually a mixture of rosin and turpentine. Rosin is brittle and remains solid at most temperatures. By use of proper kiln-drying techniques, turpentine can generally be driven out of the wood, leaving only the solid rosin. However, for green lumber or oven-dried lumber marketed for general construction, different kiln schedules may be used, and the turpentine will remain in the wood mixed with the rosin. This resin melts at a much lower temperature than does pure rosin, and consequently the mixture can migrate to the surface. If the surface has a finish, the resin may exude through the coating or cause it to discolor or blister. This usually occurs slowly, as temperature changes force the resin outward. The most serious problem occurs when the wood is heated, for example, when the sun strikes the south side of a house. Once the resin, which is sticky, is on the surface, the turpentine evaporates, leaving beads of hard rosin. If the wood is stained or painted, the rosin will diffuse through the film, discoloring it.

Power washer—Machine that boosts pressure of water supplied by a garden hose and allows you to control a high-powered stream of water that can be used in cleaning all kinds of surfaces, including wood.

Respirator—Breathing mask that allows you to spray paint or stain without breathing the fumes.

Ring orientation—The way a board is sawn, or manufactured, from a log, which affects the orientation of the annual rings and the wood's paintability. Softwood lumber is referred to as either flat-grained or edge-grained; plainsawn or quarter-sawn in hardwoods; or a combination of these. Most standard lumber is flat-grained. For example, most board-and-batten and shiplap are flat-grained. Bevel siding and redwood or cedar are generally produced in a flat-grained standard grade and an edge-grained premium grade. The problem is with the flat-grained wood. It shrinks more than edge-grained wood and has wider, darker bands of latewood. Therefore, edge-grained lumber used for siding will usually hold paint better than flat-grained, and quarter-sawn or hardwood paints hold better than plain-sawn boards. But the difference is relatively small compared to quarter-sawn and plain-sawn softwoods.

Semitransparent stain—Penetrating stain that contains more pigment than any other stain except solid color (which is really more like a flat paint). Semitransparent stains allow the grain of the wood to show.

Sleeve—Painter's term for a paint roller.

Solid-color stain—Stain that is essentially a flat paint and has a flat finish. It's big advantage over paint is that it has much less tendency to peel.

Stain—Refers to penetrating or solid-color stain.

Tannin bleed—Migration of water-soluble chemicals to the surface of wood.

Thinner—The liquid used to thin and clean up paint. For oil-based paint or stain the thinner is mineral spirits; for latex paints, it is water.

Toner—Clear finish with a slight amount of pigment.

UV blockers—Chemicals in a clear penetrating finish that block the rays of the sun.

Vehicle—The liquid portion of paint that carries the solids, such as pigment.

Viscosity—The thickness of a paint or stain.

VOC—Volatile organic compound. Carbon compound that evaporates. VOCs are found in oil-based paints. Because of their destructive effects on the environment, they have been seriously limited.

Wet edge—Important concept in paintings and staining; refers to painting sections that overlap while edges are still wet. If an edge dries and you go over it with wet stain or paint, you can get a lap mark.

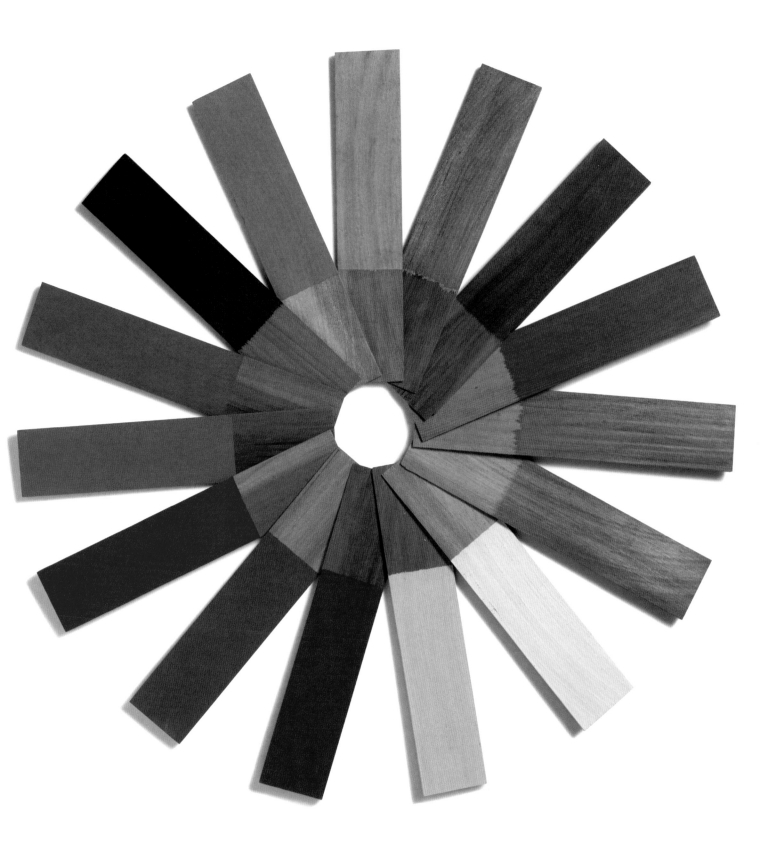

Resources

Use these phone numbers, websites, and/or email addresses to locate stain dealers in your area and find answers to specific questions about the manufacturers' products. Most of the companies listed also make various stain removers and wood cleaners.

Stain Manufacturers

Behr Process Corp
Phone: 800-854-0133, ext. 2
www.behr.com

BIO-WASH
Phone: 800-663-9274
http://biowash.com

Cabot
Phone: 800-US-STAIN
www.cabotstain.com

Flood
Phone: 800-321-3444
www.floodco.com

ICI Paints (WoodPride Professional Wood Finishes)
Phone: 800-984-5444
www.icipaints.com

Penofin
Phone: 800-736-6348 (800-PENOFIN; in United States)
www.penofin.com

PPG Industries (Olympic)
Phone: 800-441-9695
www.ppg.com/ppgaf/olympic/exterior.htm

Sherwin-Williams (WoodScapes)
Phone: 800-622-8468
www.sherwin-williams.com

The Thompson's Company
Phone: 800-367-6297
www.thompsonsonline.com

Wolman Woodcare Products
Phone: 800-556-7737
www.wolman.com

WM Barr (Strippers only)
Phone: 800-398-3892
klnstrp@wmbarr.com

Ladders

Werner Ladders
www.wernerladder.com
info@wernerladder.com

Power Washers

Alfred Kaercher
Phone: 678-935-4545
support@us.kaercher.com

Coleman
Phone: 800-4451805
www.colemanpowermate.com

DeVilbiss
Phone: 800-888-2468

Applicators

Besst Liebco Corp.
Phone: 800-523-9095
Website: www.besttliebco.com/
Email: customerservice@besstcorp.com

Graco
Phone: 800-543-0339
www.graco.com
customerservice@graco.com

Padco
Phone: 800-328-5513
www.padco.com

Purdy
Phone: 503-286-8217
www.purdycorp.com
info@purdycorp.com

Patchers

Minwax
askminwax@sherwin.com

3M
Phone: 800-494-3552
www.3m.com

Associations

California Redwood Association
Phone: 888-225-7339
info@calredwood.org

National Paint & Coatings Association
Phone: 202-462-6272
www.paint.org
npca@paint.org

Portland Cement Association
Phone: 847-966-6200
info@cement.org

USDA Forest Service
Forest Products Laboratory
Mailroom forest products
www.fs.fed.us/r4/2002/team/fpl.html
laboratory@fs.fed.us

Tools

Hyde Tools, Inc.
Phone: 800-872-4933
www.hydetools.com
info@hydetools.com

Warner Tools
Phone: 877-WARNER1
www.warnertools.com

Photographer Credits

Courtesy of Behr Process Corporation, 12; 19 (top); 82; 117; 118

Courtesy of Flood Company, 40; 90 (bottom left)

Courtesy of Graco, 50; 100; 101; 102

Courtesy of Hyde Tools, Inc., 54; 55; 59; 61 (left); 70; 75; 77 (top)

Courtesy of ICI Paints, 10; 62; 88; 96; 106

Douglas Keister, 18; 20; 25; 35; 111; 121

Rob Melnychuk, 71

Courtesy of Padco, 49; 99

Allan Penn, 23; 24; 131

Courtesy of Penofin, 90 (top); 90 (bottom right); 91 (left)

Thomas Philbin III, 42; 45; 64; 76; 77 (bottom); 83; 84; 85

Eric Roth, 6

Courtesy of Sherwin-Williams, 15

Courtesy of The Thompson's Company, 14 (left); 16; 19 (bottom); 91 (right); 103; 115; 116

Courtesy of USDA Forest Service, Forest Products Laboratory, 22

Brian Vanden Brink, 44; 51

Brian Vanden Brink/Stephen Blatt Architects, 8

Brian Vanden Brink/Bullock & Co. Log Home Builders, 104 (bottom)

Brian Vanden Brink/Roc Caivano, Architect, 38

Brian Vanden Brink/Centerbrook Architects, 2

Brian Vanden Brink/Stephen Foote, Perry Dean Rogers Partners Architects, 73

Brian Vanden Brink/Chris Glass, Architect, 58

Brian Vanden Brink/Warren Hall, Architect, 57

Brian Vanden Brink/Heartwood Log Homes, 104 (top)

Brian Vanden Brink/Horiuchi & Solien Landscape Architects, 94

Brian Vanden Brink/Mark Hutker & Associates Architects, 114

Brian Vanden Brink/Dominic Mercadante, Architect, 48

Brian Vanden Brink/John Morris Architects/John Gillespie, Project Architect, 43

Brian Vanden Brink/Lyman Perry Architects, 80

Brian Vanden Brink/Winton Scott Architects, 46

Brian Vanden Brink/Jack Silverio, Architect, 86

Brian Vanden Brink/Scott Simons, Architect, 60

Brian Vanden Brink/South Mountain Company Builders, 5

Brian Vanden Brink/Van Dam and Renner Architects, 41

Brian Vanden Brink/Weatherend Estate Furniture, 93; 112

Brian Vanden Brink/Rob Whitten, Architect, 52; 66; 68; 108

Brian Vanden Brink/Carol Wilson, Architect, 38

Courtesy of Wolman Woodcare Products, 14 (right); 61 (right); 74; 79; 110